ISLAM

ISLAM
An Introduction

Annemarie Schimmel

State University of New York Press

First published in U.S.A. by
State University of New York Press, Albany

© 1992 State University of New York

Annemarie Schimmel: Der Islam. Eine Einführung
© 1990 Philipp Reclam jun. GmbH & Co., Stuttgart

Printed in the United States of America

For information, address State University of New York Press,
State University Plaza, Albany, NY 12246

Production by Marilyn P. Semerad
Marketing by Theresa A. Swierzowski

Library of Congress Cataloging-in-Publication Data

Schimmel, Annemarie.
   [Islam. English]
   Islam : an introduction / Annemarie Schimmel.
      p.   cm.
   Translation of: Der Islam.
   Includes index.
   ISBN 0-7914-1327-6 (hardcover). —
   ISBN 0-7914-1328-4 (paper)
   1. Islam—History.   I. Title.
BP55.S3413   1992
297—dc20   92-2558
                                   CIP

10 9 8 7 6 5 4

How strange that in every special case
one praises one's own way!
If Islam means "surrender into God's will"
it's in Islam that we all live and die.

Johann Wolfgang von Goethe

Contents

Introduction

Among all the religions which Christianity had to confront and deal with, Islam was both misunderstood and attacked most intensely. For more than a millenium Islam seemed to be a major—if not the major—threat for the people of Europe, and this feeling has contributed to the fact that Islam and those who confessed it, the Muslims, were regarded as arch enemies of Christianity and western civilization. On the political level this threat began with the conquest of Spain by the Arabs at the beginning of the eighth century and it ended with the siege of Vienna by the Ottoman Turks in 1683.

But there were not only political reasons for Christian Europe's fear: Islam is the only world religion that came into existence after Christianity, and was hence unacceptable as a true religion. Often it was considered to be a mere heresy of Christianity, an attitude first found in early Byzantine apologetic writings and continuing for centuries; this attitude was later expressed by the German theologian Adolf von Harnack (d. 1930) and can be observed occasionally in our own day.

The medieval European image of Islam and of its Prophet, Muhammad, is a thoroughly distorted one. The distortion reached such absurdities as to consider Muhammad, usually called Mahomet (hence the Scottish *Mahound* for "devil"), to be a kind of "supreme god" and to speak of the adoration of his golden statues. The image of the *goldne Mahomsbilder,* golden effigies of Muhammad, continued to be used in early nineteenth-century German romantic poetry.

The fact that a religion which refuses even the smallest trace of idolatry and whose prophet regarded himself as nothing but a human being, a servant of the one and unique God, could be misinterpreted to such an extent is partly due to lack of linguistic knowledge. Not before the early fourteenth century was the knowledge of Arabic, the cultic and theological language of Islam, considered worthy of special instruction in southern European universities. (In Muslim Spain, however, Christian clerics were perfectly familiar with the language of the rulers.)

In 1143, the first Latin translation of the Koran was produced by Robertus Ketenensis; exactly four centuries later, this very translation (which included a refutation) of the sacred scripture of Islam was printed in Basel by Bibliander at the instigation of Martin Luther. Based on this translation, an Italian translation appeared, and then, in 1616, a German translation by Salomon Schweigger; this was soon followed by a Dutch translation.

During this period a few rare scholars began to show interest in the Arabic language without missionary aims. But despite the slowly increasing familiarity with Arabic history and the languages of Islam, in the sixteenth and seventeenth centuries a number of books of decidedly anti-Islamic character were produced, undoubtedly related to the pressure of the Turkish presence in eastern Europe. Many poetical products of this time reflect the boundless hatred, particularly of German writers, for the 'Turkish religion.'

During the Enlightenment there slowly emerged a new approach to religions, including Islam. For the first time, Henri de Boulainvilliers (1658–1722) portrayed Muhammad as a man who preached a religion based on and conforming to reason. The attitude of enlightened scholars of this period is expressed probably best by Hermann Samuel Reimarus (1694–1768) who wrote:

> I am convinced that among those who accuse the Turkish religion of this or that fault, only a very few have read the Alcoran and that also among those who indeed have read it only a precious few have had the intention to give the words the sound meaning of which they are capable.

By this time a translation of the Koran by the British scholar George Sale had appeared (1734). Sale's judgment concerning the Koran was more matter of fact and to the point than that of his predecessors, who always found it necessary to apologize for translating the Koran at all. The first German translation from the original Arabic was that of David Friedrich Megerlin (1772), which was used by Goethe. One year later, another German translation appeared, this one by Friedrich Eberhard Boysen.

The indefatigable Johann Jacob Reiske (1715–1774), called by his friends "the martyr of Arabic Literature," was the first to undertake the task of integrating Islamic history into universal history. The classical attitude, which concluded the West's centuries-old critical if not inimical preoccupation with Islam, is expressed in Goethe's *Noten und Abhandlungen zum West-Östlichen Divan* (1818). Cautiously and with due justice he attempts to describe not only Muhammad's personality but also the essence of Islamic culture as expressed in its main forms, Arabic and Persian.

Goethe, to be sure, came at the end of a period during which the Islamic East had fertilized Western culture in spite of political and theological feuds. It is possible to trace literary and artistic influences in medieval Spain, where representatives of Arabic natural sciences brought invaluable treasures to medieval Europe. Eastern influences can also be discovered in stories and romantic tales and poems of the Middle Ages. The Crusades supplied the

West with precious goods, and words such as *damast, baldachin, muslin, lute,* and many more (including *tabby*) give evidence of the Arabic origin of luxury items that reached Europe during those centuries. Many names of stars (Aldebaran, Betelgeuse) and mathematical terms (algorithmus, algebra) as well as chemical expressions (alchemy, alcohol) are part of the Arabic scientific heritage.

Later, travelers to the Ottoman Empire, to Iran, and to India, then ruled by the Great Mughals, gave reports of the splendor and wealth of these countries. They also introduced Persian literary works into Germany: a typical example is the German translation by Adam Olearius of Saʿdi's *Gulistān* (1653).

"Thanks to us, Persia enters Holstein in state!" Thus wrote Paul Fleming, a member of the embassy to Iran from Schleswig-Holstein-Gottorp, a small principality in northern Germany. And indeed, despite Daniel Caspar Lohenstein's abominably cruel anti-Turkish dramas, the Orient was now regarded no longer only as the home of the Antichrist but also as a fairyland filled with wonders, the source of the tales of the Arabian Nights. At the beginning of the eighteenth century, these tales were translated into French by Antoine Galland. This rather free adaptation inspired numerous poets, musicians, and painters, and it continues to do so to this day.

Toward the end of the eighteenth century, the first examples of classical Oriental poetry became known in Europe. Joseph von Hammer-Purgstall (1774–1856) deserves high credit for his translations into German of innumerable works from Arabic, Persian, and Turkish. Hammer's translation of the complete *Divan* of Hafiz, which appeared in 1812–1813, inspired Goethe to compose his *West-Östlicher Divan,* the first Western poetical response to a masterpiece of Persian lyrics. We further owe to Hammer-Purgstall major historical works such as the *History of the Ottoman Empire* in ten volumes. Germany was uniquely fortunate in that one of Hammer's part-time disciples, Friedrich Rückert (1788–1866), a first-class orientalist, was at the same time a fine poet in his own right; he introduced to Germany an immense treasure of Arabic, Persian, and Indian poetry in the closest possible adaptation to the original forms and meters. After Rückert, however, literary adaptation and serious scholarly work drifted increasingly away from each other. The Anglo-Saxon world played a considerable role in the orientalist tradition, beginning with the works of the British scholars in Fort William, Calcutta (under British rule since 1757). The colonial interests of both Britain and France during the nineteenth century helped develop a rich literature descriptive of Muslim manners and customs and inspired various genres of orientalizing painting and architecture. In Germany, however, the pure, scholarly study of Islamic history, literature, and Arabic grammar was earnestly pursued.

It was in the nineteenth century that a scholarly approach to Islam began. In 1842, Gustav Weil tried to describe the life of the Prophet by separating what appeared to be historical events from later pious legends. In the following decades William Muir, the Austrian Aloys Sprenger, and D. F. Margoliouth tended to draw a rather negative picture of Muhammad, describing him as hysterical and pathological, an imposter (as previous centuries had done) or, at best, a mere social reformer.

While the German Theodor Nöldeke made fundamental contributions to the history of the Koran, the Hungarian Ignaz Goldziher wrote his admirable studies concerning the development of *ḥadīth*, the different methods of interpreting the Koran, and numerous other major and minor works that have not been superseded. These two scholars, along with the Dutch Islamologist C. Snouck Hurgronje, built the foundations of scientific Islamology (*Islamwissenschaft*); they and their contemporaries and successors tried to discover the Prophet's true goal and how Islamic intellectual history unfolded. They tried to penetrate with ever-new methods the traditions, ideas, and developments that seemed to surround the religion which, though said to have been "born in the full light of history," is still shrouded in many mysteries. Carl Heinrich Becker once wrote: "We know too much of Muhammad to idealize him but too little to do full justice to him.''

The attitude of orientalists in the past century has been criticized frequently during recent decades, whether one discovers, with Edward Said, imperialistic goals in the works of British and French scholars or regrets the lack of true understanding of the spiritual aspects of Islam. During recent years, however, a considerable number of publications express their authors' warm sympathy for Islam and, in particular, for its mystical dimensions. The positive attitude of the Second Vatican Council has contributed to new efforts for better understanding of a much-maligned religion. Yet one also has to take into account extremely critical approaches to early Islam, which try to interpret early Islamic history and culture from new and unusual vantage points.

On the following pages we take the traditional view of Islamic history without venturing into the vast area of sociological or political approaches.

Arabia Before Islam

South Arabia, the *Arabia felix* of antiquity, had been famed for its wealth, but when Muhammad was born (570) its most glorious times were over. Ancient polytheism had been largely replaced by Jewish and Christian influences. In Central Arabia, a rather "primitive" religion was still maintained, and the country boasted numerous tribal sanctuaries. Caves and (as is common among the Semites) stones were regarded as sacred and filled with blessing power, *baraka*. A center of the stone cult was Mecca: there, the black stone in the southeastern corner of the Ka'ba was the goal of annual pilgrimages. Such pilgrimages, performed at specific times, brought the wealthy trade center economic advantages. Trade fairs and markets were held during the four sacred months, during which fighting and killing were prohibited, and members of all Arabic clans and tribes would travel to the sacred places. The life of the Arabs during that period, which the Muslims call *jāhiliyya,* "time of ignorance," showed but little trace of deep religious feeling, as far as one can judge from inscriptions and

7

literature. Arabic literature (primarily poetry) from the late sixth century A.D. sings mainly of the virtues of the Bedouins: that is, bravery, boundless hospitality, revenge, faith in an immutable fate, but does not display much religious consciousness. Compared with the themes of heroic life, the purely erotic moment remains in the background. The women of the tribe used to compose threnodies for those slain in war; the priests at the sanctuaries performed soothsaying in high-sounding rhyming prose.

It is astounding to see how highly developed the Arabic language already was at this early time. In its poetical idiom, which was common to all tribes, it unfolded to perfection the finest tendencies inherent in all Semitic languages, superseding the dialectical variants of everyday speech. An almost inexhaustible wealth of words is combined with an extreme syntactic brevity, and even at that early time the use of several distinct meters in poetry can be seen. In fact, the perfection of pre-Islamic Arabic poetry has rarely been reached by writers at any later point in history, and the language, with its apparently boundless possibilities, was perhaps the most important and precious heritage which Islam received from its native Arabic soil.

Now and then in ancient Arabic poetry, Christian motifs appear: wandering monks, or the light that shines forth from a hermit's cell. The country was situated in the sphere of influence of Byzanz and Persia, both trade partners of the Meccans, and this facilitated contacts with Jacobite, Melkite, and Nestorian Christians; but entire Christian colonies would probably not have been found in the heart of Arabia. However, there were Jewish settlements not far from Medina; furthermore, the kings of Sheba had converted to Judaism around the year 500. One hears also of seekers, unsatisfied with the dominant religion of the Arabs, who were in quest of a higher faith. These men were called *ḥanīf*, and it seems that the belief in a high God, *Allāh* (a term that incidentally appears elsewhere among the Arabs) formed the center of their religious attitude. It may well be that their religious interest had been intensified by contacts with Christians or Jews. One can speculate that Arabia possibly would have become a Christian country during the late sixth to early seventh century, had Muhammad not appeared on the scene.

Muhammad

Muhammad was born about 570 in Mecca as a member of the Hashim clan of the Quraish, to which most of the notables of Mecca belonged. He lost his parents early (his father died before his birth) and he was brought up by his uncle, Abu Talib. Like most of his Meccan compatriots, he devoted himself to trade. After some successful journeys to Syria the young Muhammad, called *al-Amīn* for his reliability, married his employer, Khadija, who was his senior by several years. She bore him several children, among whom four daughters survived; all but one predeceased their father. Muhammad did not marry any other woman as long as Khadija was alive (she died when he was about fifty years old). This fact certainly does not support the prejudice commonly vented in the West, where he was regarded as extremely sensual due to his numerous later marriages, which particularly upset those who espoused the ideal of celibacy.

Muhammad liked to retire at times to meditate in a cave in Mt. Hira, and when he was about forty years old, he

11

was overcome by visions and even more by voices. It took
him some time to realize that it was an angelic voice that
was entrusting him with a divine mandate. Sura 96 of the
Koran contains the first such address, *iqra*ʾ ("Read" or
"Recite!") and thus points to the groundbreaking experience. Khadija faithfully supported her husband in the spiritual crises triggered by these experiences.

The first proclamations preached by Muhammad are
dominated by one single thought: the nearing Day of Judgment. The terrible shock caused by the sudden approach of
the Hour, the Day of Reckoning, and the resurrection is
heralded by breathless short lines in sonorous rhymed
prose. Close is this Hour. In a short while it will knock at
the door and will stir up from heedlessness those who are
embroiled in worldly affairs and who have forgotten God!
Then they will have to face their Lord to give account of
their sinful actions. Natural catastrophes will announce the
Day of Judgment—earthquakes, fires, eclipses—as described in Sura 81 in unforgettable words:

> When the sun shall be darkened,
> when the stars shall be thrown down,
> when the mountains shall be set moving,
> when the pregnant camels shall be neglected,
> when the savage beasts shall be mustered,
> when the seas shall be set boiling,
> when the souls shall be coupled,
> when the buried infant shall be asked for what sin she
>   was slain,
> when the scrolls shall be unrolled,
> when heaven shall be stripped off,
> when Hell shall be set blazing,
> when Paradise shall be brought nigh,
> then shall a soul know what it has produced.
>   (translated by A. J. Arberry)

At that hour Israfil will blow the trumpet; the dead
will be resurrected in the body and, in complete confusion,
will ask each other about their fate. Certain trials have to be
faced, and finally the unbelievers and sinners will be

dragged away by their feet and their forelocks. The Koranic descriptions of Judgment and Hell do not reach the fantastic descriptions of, for example, Christian apocalyptic writing. Later popular piety, however, could never get enough detail of all kinds of chastisement; of terrible pain in the fire; of stinking, hot, or dirty water; of the fruits of poisonous trees; and of various tortures.

But Muhammad learned that he was not only sent to threaten and blame, but also to bring good tidings: every pious man who lives according to God's order will enter Paradise where rivers of milk and honey flow in cool, fragrant gardens and virgin beloveds await him. Women and children too participate in the paradisial bliss. In its description of Paradise, so often attacked by Christian polemists because of its sensuality, the Koran is not much more colorful than were the sermons on this topic in the Eastern orthodox church.

The practical-minded Meccan merchants did not take Muhammad's message seriously; to them a corporeal resurrection seemed both impossible and ludicrous. To refute their doubts, the Koran brings forth numerous proofs for such a resurrection. First, it cannot be difficult for God, who has created the world out of nothing, to reunite the already existing parts and particles. Second, a revivication of the—apparently—dead desert after rainfall is a symbol of the quickening of human beings. This reasoning was used time and again in later didactic and mystical poetry: for those who have eyes to see, every spring proves the resurrection. Finally, human fertility and birth can be taken as signs of God's unlimited creative power: the growth of a fertilized egg into a perfect living being is certainly no less miraculous than the resurrection of the dead. Furthermore, the judgments meted out to sinful peoples of the past and the calamities that wiped out ancient nations should be proof enough of how God deals with sinners as well as with those who reject the prophets sent to them, thus contributing to their own annihilation.

As the creation and the Last Judgment are closely related to each other, it is logical that the Creator and the

Lord of Doomsday must be one and the same. The belief in one God, without partners and without adjunct deities, forms the center of the revelation from an early moment onward. Sura 112 declares:

> Say: God is One; God the Eternal: He did not beget and is not begotten, and no one is equal to Him.

This *sura*, which is nowadays used mainly to refute the Christian trinitarian dogma, was probably first directed against the ancient Arab concept of 'the daughters of Allah.' But the *tauḥīd*, the acknowledgment of God's unity, was to remain the heart of Islam, in whichever way it was understood, and the only sin that cannot be forgiven is *shirk*, "associating something with God."

The duty of human beings is to surrender to this unique, omnipotent God, the Merciful, the Compassionate (as He is called at the beginning of each chapter of the Koran and also at the beginning of every human activity); to surrender from the bottom of one's heart, with one's whole soul and one's entire mind. The word "Islam" means this complete surrender to the Divine will; and the one who practices such surrender is a Muslim (active participle of the fourth stem of the root *s.l.m.*, which has also the connotation of *salām*, "peace"). Muslims do not like the term "Muhammedan," as it suggests an incorrect parallel to the way Christians call themselves after Christ. Only members of some late mystical currents called themselves *Muḥammadī* to express their absolute loyalty to the Prophet as their spiritual and temporal leader.

The Muslim, who recognizes the One God as both Creator and Judge, feels responsible to Him: he believes in His books (the Torah, the Psalms, the Gospels, and the Koran) and in His prophets from Adam through the patriarchs, Moses, and Jesus up to Muhammad, the last lawgiving messenger. Further, he believes in God's angels and in the Last Judgment, and "that good and evil come equally from God." He tries to lead his life according to the revealed law, well aware that God's presence is experienced in every

place and every time, and that there is no really profane
sphere in life. Fulfillment of cultic duties and the practice
of mercy and justice are commanded side by side in the Koran: the ritual prayer, *ṣalāt,* is in almost every instance
combined with *zakāt,* the alms tax. But the worldlings who
are embroiled in caring for their wealth, and who neglect
religious duties, are threatened by Divine punishment.

Muhammad saw himself at first as a messenger to the
Arabs: he was sent to warn them, as no prophet had been
sent to them since Abraham. However, only a comparatively small circle of adherents, mainly from the lower
classes, gathered around him. The situation did not im-
prove, for the doctrine of the One Supreme God seemed to
threaten the main sources of income for the Meccans, i.e.,
the fairs in honor of various deities and especially the pilgrimage. With the hostility of the Meccans increasing, a
group of the new Muslims emigrated to Abyssinia, a Christian country. The situation grew even more difficult after
Muhammad, in 619, lost both his wife and his uncle Abu
Talib, who, although not converted to Islam, had supported
his nephew faithfully. However, new possibilities arose in
621: some inhabitants of Yathrib, north of Mecca, came to
perform religious rites and invited Muhammad to join them
in their home town, which was torn by internal feuds. After
his faithful companions had left Mecca, Muhammad himself, along with his friend Abu Bakr, migrated in June 622
to settle in Yathrib, which soon became known as *madīnat
an-nabī,* "the city of the Prophet," or Medina.

The Muslims consider their era to have begun with the
date of this emigration (*hijra* or hegira), for at this point a
decisive development of Muhammad's activities can be observed: the religious vision of the Meccan revelations had
now to be put into communal practice. Furthermore, up to
this time the Prophet had considered himself merely as a
continuator of the great prophetic religions, Judaism and
Christianity. He was convinced that he was preaching the
same truth that Jews and Christians had been teaching and
practicing. Stories known to us from the Bible can be found
in the Koran; thus, Sura 12 contains what it calls "the most

beautiful story," that of Joseph and his brothers and
Potiphar's wife (called Zulaikha in the later tradition), a
topic that was to inspire innumerable poets in the Muslim
world. However, the Jews refused to accept the revelations
connected to their own traditions, for these seemed not to
tally completely with the biblical words and to have many
gaps. Their objections led Muhammad to the conviction
that the Jews had tampered with the revelations in their
scripture. He concluded that only the version revealed to
him contained the true and real text of these stories and that
the faith preached by him on the basis of direct revelation
was much older than that professed by the Jews and Christians; his was the pure faith of Abraham who, through
Isma'il (Ishmael), is the ancestor of the Arabs and who is
said to have founded the central sanctuary in Mecca, the
Ka'ba. Pure monotheism, as represented for the first time
by Abraham, a *hanif* who had refuted his ancestors' stellar
religion, had been corrupted by Jews and Christians and
should now become alive again in Islam.

In keeping with this perception of Islam's connection
to Abraham, the direction of prayer, till then toward Jerusalem, was changed to Mecca; this made necessary the
conquest of Mecca. Eight years after his migration, Muhammad entered his home town in triumph. During these
eight years a number of battles were fought: in Badr, 624, a
small group of Muslims encountered a strong Meccan army
and was victorious, while one year later the Meccans
gained a slim victory near Uhud. Three Jewish tribes were
overcome and partially uprooted. The Meccans were dis-
quieted by the growing success of their compatriot, but they
finally were forced to let him return. He forgave most of
those who had worked and plotted against him, but he pre-
ferred to stay in Medina. There he eventually died after performing the rites of the pilgrimage in 632. After Khadija's
death Muhammad had married several wives (mainly wid-
ows); his favorite wife, however, was the young 'A'isha, a
mere child when he married her. He passed away in her
house, and her father Abu Bakr aṣ-Ṣiddīq, "the very faithful one," became his first successor, or "caliph."

The revelations that came upon Muhammad during the last decade of his life are stylistically quite different from the earlier ones: the rhyming prose is less conspicuous and the fiery eschatological threats have given way to discussion of cultic and institutional problems, for Muhammad's role as arbiter and community leader required legal injunctions and rules for the political and social structure of the nascent community. All of life was and is permeated by religion, and just as there is no clear separation between the political and religious aspects of communal life, there are no truly profane acts either. Every act has to begin with the words "in the name of God," *bismillāh,* and must be performed in responsibility to God. The human being stands immediately before God; no mediating priestly caste exists.

The Expansion of Islam

Muhammad's death confronted the young community with difficult problems. The office of prophet no longer existed, for the revelation (Sura 33/40) had spoken of Muhammad as the 'seal', the last of the prophets. His successors, *khalīfa*, (caliphs) inherited only the office of leading the community in prayer and war and judging according to the revelation.

This community, *umma*, consists of the believers and is, as legend attests, especially protected by its relation to Muhammad. For, thus it is told, at Doomsday when everybody (including the sinless Jesus) will be exclaiming: *nafsī nafsī* ("I myself, I myself [want to be saved]"), Muhammad will call: *Ummatī, ummatī* ("my community, my community [should be saved]") and thus act as intercessor, *shafīʿ*, for his community, an idea that has consoled Muslims throughout the centuries.

Abu Bakr, the father of the Prophet's wife ʿAʾisha and his first successor, managed to overcome the rebellions that broke out soon after Muhammad's death, for the freedom-loving Bedouins, who particularly disliked the Islamic

tax system, tried to regain their old independence. During
Abu Bakr's short reign (632–634), the armies of the Muslims reached southern Iraq and Palestine. These enterprises
can be explained when one remembers that in 628—so tradition has it—the Prophet had sent letters to the rulers of
Byzanz, Iran, and Egypt to invite them to embrace Islam.
Shortly afterwards, first encounters with the Byzantines
took place. This opened the way for his successors to further conquests, and military success of spectacular scope
was achieved under Abu Bakr's successor, the stern ʿUmar
ibn al-Khattab (634–644). Damascus was conquered in
635, Egypt in 639–644, and most of Persia between 640
and 644.

After ʿUmar's assassination in 644, ʿUthman ibn
ʿAffan (644–656) successfully continued sending out Muslim armies east and west. Members of the ancient aristo-
cratic Meccan family Umayya now reappeared at the political forefront, although this very family had been among
Muhammad's staunchest opponents. Some of those disaf-
fected with the new regime rose against ʿUthman, who was
murdered in 656 while reading the Koran; it was he who
was responsible for the final redaction of the sacred book.
ʿAli the son of Muhammad's uncle Abu Talib and husband
of his youngest daughter Fatima, became ʿUthman's successor, but had to fight Muʿawiya, from the house of
Umayya. In the battle of Siffin, 657, Muʿawiya persuaded
ʿAli to stop fighting (though ʿAli was about to gain victory)
and to submit himself to arbitration. A segment of ʿAli's
partisans, outraged at his acceptance of this proposal, left
ʿAli (they are known as Kharijites, "seceders"); in 661, a
Kharijite assassinated ʿAli, and Muʿawiya, understandably,
took advantage of his death.

With Muʿawiya begins the Umayyad dynasty, whose
rulers resided in Syria to reign in the spirit of traditional
Arabic leadership and chivalry, while Medina turned into
the repository of piety without political power. Under the
Umayyads the Muslims extended their rule to the Atlantic
in 691; they reached the borders of Byzantium, and their
armies crossed the Straits of Gibraltar (*Jabal Ṭāriq,* the

mountain of Tariq) in 711. During the same year they entered Transoxiana and also conquered Sind, the lower Indus Valley (now the southern part of Pakistan).

When Muʿawiya's son Yazid took power in 680, ʿAli's younger son Husain, then in his late fifties, tried once more to regain power for his house. After all, was he not the legitimate grandson of the Prophet? His elder brother, Hasan, had perished more than a decade earlier (possibly poisoned), although he had forfeited his claims to the caliphate. Husain, his companions, and members of his family were killed in the battle of Kerbela in southern Iraq, on 10 Muharram (the first month of the Islamic year). The anniversary of his death is to this day a day of mourning in the Shiite world; his suffering has inspired hundreds of pious poets to compose moving threnodies, *marthiya*, especially in Persian and Urdu. The processions in Shiite cities in Iran and India, with people flagellating themselves, are well known; in Iran, regular "passion plays" are performed. It is this passion motif which has shaped Shiite piety and deeply permeates it, and many of the recent events in Iran—such as the passionate participation of so many people in the war against "the enemies of the faith"—can be explained by this feeling of loyalty to Husain, the arch martyr of Islam. Husain's struggle against the Umayyad regime was regarded both in high literature and popular piety as an expression of the Muslims' longing for freedom, for liberation from unjust rulers, and, in later times (especially in British India), from foreign powers that oppress believers.

At the same time a counter-caliph appeared in Mecca. ʿAbdullah ibn Zubair, son of a well-known companion of the Prophet, rebelled against the Umayyads. As for Iraq, where the party of ʿAli, *shīʿat ʿAli*, was in any case the strongest political force, new doctrines developed. Ideas appeared concerning the future return of some Alids, who now were living in the hidden world, and grew into a large body of speculations in both theology and folk piety in the centuries to come. Again in Iraq, relations between the Arab conquerors and the *mawālī* (non-Arabs who were attached to an Arabic tribe as clients in order to be full

members of the Muslim community) grew tense, for the
mawālī understandably requested the complete equality of
believers, as guaranteed by the Koran.

All these different currents formed a movement whose
representatives requested the office of caliph for members
of Muhammad's clan only. The propagandists of this movement very skillfully used the pro-Alid feeling in Iraq and
Iran to enthrone as caliph a descendant of the Prophet's uncle ʿAbbas (749), thus deeply disappointing the partisans of
ʿAli's children.

The last Umayyad fled to Andalusia where he
founded, in 756, a kingdom which was to produce the finest flowers of Arabic culture in art and poetry. The
Spanish-Umayyad kingdom reached its culmination under
ʿAbdur Rahman III (912–961). It continued until 1031, wit-
nessing a unique cultural cooperation between Muslims,
Christians, and Jews. After 1031 the country fell to pieces,
and Berber groups—the Almohads and the Almoravids—
entered the Iberian peninsula to rule there while the Spanish reconquest increased in strength year by year. The only
kingdom able to survive till 1492 was that of the Banu Ah-
mar in Granada; the Alhambra is the last work of Arabic art
in Spain.

As for the Abbasid rulers, they tried to prove their ad-
herence to religious law more than their predecessors had
done. More importantly, the empire they ruled was no
longer meant to be Arab, as it had been under the Umayyads, but rather was intended to be Islamic. The transfer of
the capital from Damascus to Baghdad in 756 opened all
doors to Persian cultural influence, and when the external
power of the caliphs decreased in the late ninth century,
Turkish mercenaries and war slaves (*mamlūks*) from Central Asia protected the government and finally founded
kingdoms of their own.

Baghdad lived through its most splendid period under
Harun ar-Rashid (786–809), well known from the tales of
the Arabian Nights. Under Harun's second son Maʾmun
(813–833), translations of Greek scientific and philosophical works into Arabic were encouraged. These translations

influenced the development of Islamic learning and were later transferred to Europe, enriched by Arabic contributions; these works, through the mediation of translators in medieval Spain, helped the growth of European science and medicine.

Slightly later, princes in the border areas of the Abbasid empire moved toward independence, taking their realms as fiefs from the caliph. The founder of the Persian Shiite dynasty of the Buwaihids (Buyids), Mu'izz ad-Daula, adopted the title "sultan" for the first time (932). In 945, the Buwaihids took over actual rule in Baghdad, with the caliph continuing to serve as the figure head.

In Egypt, two Turkish dynasties succeeded each other as supporters of the Abbasids. They were ousted in 969 when the Shiite Fatimids conquered the country, coming from North Africa to found Cairo.

In the east, the Turkish sultan Mahmud of Ghazna extended his power into the Indian subcontinent; in 1026 Lahore became the capital of the Indian province of the Ghaznavids. From that time a rich Persian literature and Persianate culture developed in the subcontinent, extending to Bengal and southern India, the Deccan. Shortly before the Ghaznavids, a new era of neo-Persian as the language of literature had begun in Khorasan, present-day Afghanistan, thanks to the literary interests of the princely house of the Samanids. Although Arabic remained the sacred, theological language of the Islamic world, Persian was accepted as the main literary medium in the areas that stretched from the Balkans to Bengal, even though at a later point Turkish became an important literary medium, while in the subcontinent diverse regional languages slowly began to bloom.

While Mahmud and his successors consolidated their empire, other Turkish groups from Central Asia entered Iran and Iraq, and in 1055 the Seljuk prince Tughrul Beg assumed the role of guardian of the weak Abbasid caliph. The Seljuks, stern Sunnites, formed one of the most important empires in the Near East and inspired new developments in Islamic art. In 1071, their victory over the

Byzantines opened the way into Anatolia for the Muslims. To this day one can admire the grand mosques, madrasahs, and mausoleums built by the Rum Seljuks or their suzerains in Erzerum, Sivas, Kaiseri, and their residence, Konya. Their realm extended to the southern coastal area of Anatolia.

Much of the flourishing Islamic civilization was wiped out by the Mongol onslaught, which began in Central Asia in 1220, and to which the Abbasid Empire succumbed; the last caliph was killed in 1258, and Baghdad was largely destroyed. In Anatolia the Rum Seljuk empire disintegrated under Mongol pressure. Out of the numerous independent principalities, the family of the Ottomans emerged as leaders, and under Orhan, the second ruler of this house, Bursa was conquered in 1326. This city on the northwestern fringe of Anatolia became the first cultural center of the nascent Ottoman Empire. After the battle of Kosova in Yugoslavia in 1389, large parts of the Balkans came under Ottoman rule; the new capital was Edirne (Adrianople). But when Constantinople, Istanbul, was conquered on May 29, 1453, it became the heart of the Empire. Did not the Prophet say: "They will conquer Constantinople—hail to the people and hail to the army who will do so!"

The Mongol rule, some of whose rulers converted to Islam about 1300, gave new impulses to the areas of Iran and Iraq, which had been lacking a central authority since 1258, even though the caliphs had long ceased wielding real power. Following the Mongol conquest a number of principalities emerged in Iran, many of which were overrun by Timur (Tamerlane), the Turkish conqueror from Central Asia (d. 1405). He reached northwestern India as far as Delhi in 1398, and Ankara in central Anatolia in 1402. An extremely cruel warrior, Tamerlane was nevertheless interested in fine art and literature, took with him master craftsmen from everywhere he went, and had his capital, Samarkand, adorned with beautiful buildings. His descendants, especially those who ruled the eastern part of the Iranian world, were likewise patrons of fine art. Miniature painting as well as calligraphy reached their first highpoint in the late fifteenth century in Herat, and poetry flourished.

As for Egypt, the Fatimid, Shia-Ismaili dynasty had been replaced after 200 years of rule by the Sunnite Kurdish family of the Ayyubids. The most important ruler of this dynasty was Saladin, famed even in Europe as a just and noble ruler, thanks to his role during the Crusades. The marriage of the widow of the last Ayyubid with her Turkish commander-in-chief led, in 1250, to the formation of the Mamluk reign in Egypt. The strong, energetic Mamluk sultan Baibars was able to stop the Mongol hordes at Ain Jalut in Syria in 1260. During the first half of the Mamluk reign, until 1382, the throne was usually hereditary, while in the second period the sultan was generally elected. The ruler had to be a member of the class of military slaves imported from southern Russia, the Kipchak steppes, or the Caucasus; a long and complicated process was required for such a slave to reach higher rungs on the ladder of military hierarchy. The Mamluk rule of Egypt, Syria, and the holy cities of Mecca and Medina is notable for building activities on a grand scale. It ended in 1516 when the Ottoman troops under Selim the Grim vanquished the Egyptian army near Marj Dabiq, north of Aleppo.

Ottoman power then extended over the Fertile Crescent and the sacred cities; under Selim's successor, Süleyman the Magnificent (1520–1566), the Ottomans proceeded even farther than before to the west to lay siege to Vienna in 1529. During Süleyman's reign the master architect Sinan adorned the capital as well as Edirne with magnificent mosques.

To the east of the Ottoman empire, Shiite movements that had been evident in Iran for some time crystallized toward the turn of the fifteenth and sixteenth centuries. In 1501, Shah Isma'il, at the age of fourteen, ascended the throne of Iran to found the dynasty of the Safavids and to make the Shiite form of Islam the official religion of Iran. Thus, a Shiite wedge was placed between the Sunni Ottomans in the West and the emerging, predominantly Sunni

Mughal Empire in the east (although Shia rulers became more prominent in India in the course of time). This religio-political situation helps explain certain developments in the Middle East and also the special role of Iran during the last decades, for the Shiite form of Islam was never made the state religion in any other country.

At the time when the Ottoman empire was expanding and Iran was becoming a Shiite country while Timur's descendants were losing their grip over eastern Iran, another member of the house of Timur, Babur, born in Farghana, founded a powerful empire in northwestern India. Ever since the inroads of Mahmud of Ghazna after the year 1000, Muslim kingdoms had followed each other in the subcontinent, extending soon to eastern Bengal and to the Deccan. Babur overcame the Lodi rulers of Delhi in 1526 to found the dynasty of the Great Mughals, which continued to exist for more than three centuries. Babur's son Humayun had to seek shelter at the Safavid court of Iran, but was able to return to his homeland and had just begun to consolidate it when he died in an accident. It was his son Akbar (1556–1605) who gave the empire its true shape. His tolerance for, interest in, and cooperation with Hindus, Christians, and Parsees colored at least part of Indian Islam. His own and his descendants' lively interest in fine arts, especially architecture and miniature painting, gave Islamic art new impulses.

Akbar's son Jahangir and his grandson, Shah Jahan followed his tolerant attitude to a certain extent. Shah Jahan's son Dara Shikoh is famed for his interest in mysticism and in the religious systems of Hinduism; he undertook a Persian translation from the Sanskrit of fifty Upanishads. The finest architectural works in northern India belong to the early Mughal time, i.e., the years between 1560 and 1660, such as the famed Taj Mahal, the mausoleum of Shah Jahan's wife. This glorious period ended with Dara Shikoh's execution in 1659 at the hand of his brother Aurangzeb, who in vain tried to expand the Mughal empire into the Deccan where the kingdoms of Bijapur and Golconda boasted a refined Islamic cultural life and were seats of literature and fine arts for more than two centuries. Aurangzeb died, aged nearly ninety, in 1707. The weakened empire became a toy for different Indian factions and assorted invaders: the Persian king Nadir Shah plundered Delhi in 1739 and the Afghan leader Ahmad Shah Durrani led military expeditions against northwest India. The political awakening of the Hindus (especially the Mahrattas) and the Sikhs and, more than anything else, the increasing expansion of the British East India Company from 1757 resulted finally in the political breakdown of the last vestiges of the Mughal empire. After the abortive military revolt, the so-called Mutiny, in 1857, the British Crown took over India with the exception of the princely states; the last Mughal emperor died in Rangoon in exile.

Islam continued to spread in the Indian and Indonesian areas even in times of political decay; nowadays almost half of the world's Muslims live in this part of the world. The first modernist movements in the nineteenth century began from the Indian subcontinent in order to help Muslims to adapt to—or to resist—modern life as they observed it in the activities of their colonial masters. One must not forget the strong, very active groups of Muslims in Central Asia and China, and the steadily growing presence of Islam in East and West Africa. The growing number of Muslims in the Western world should also be mentioned.

From the late seventeenth century, a certain stagnation among Muslims can be observed as a result of political weakness and the loss of many important areas after the opening of the sea passage to India and the rapid growth of European power. However, in the eighteenth century—a time usually neglected by orientalists—germs of new interpretations of the Koran and of Islam as well as first attempts at self-identification vis-à-vis the West become visible in different parts of the Islamic world. In the nineteenth century, some Islamic peoples reached a more outspoken form of self-assertion and attempted to define their role as Muslims in a changing world. After World War I, nationalism, inoculated into the Near and Middle East by Europeans, appears with full strength. The division of the

Middle East after that war, in the attempt to dismember the Ottoman Empire, helped the growth of nationalism. A number of independent states were formed whose names may or may not include references to Islam. The gamut, with changing emphasis, runs from the Islamic Republic of Pakistan to Turkey, which claims absolute laicism as the foundation of its constitution, even though many people still feel they are perfectly faithful Muslims. Those who know the Turkish mentality are not surprised that lately some fundamentalist movements are appearing in Turkey as in other countries. The tension between laical and fundamentalist attitudes is probably more visible there than elsewhere.

The Koran and
Its Teachings

The foundation of Islam is the Koran (*qurʾān*, "recitation") which is, for the pious Muslim, not the word of a prophet but the unadulterated word of God, which has become audible through Muhammad, the pure vessel, in "clear Arabic language." Thus, quotations from the Koran are introduced by the words *qāla taʿālā,* "He—Elevated is He—says" or similar formulas. The primordial Koran, which exists in heaven on a "well-preserved tablet," manifested itself in this book which "only the purified" are permitted to touch and to recite. To recite the Koran is the most sublime and edifying occupation for the Muslim, even when he or she does not intellectually understand its words, as is the case with most non-Arab believers. Since the Koran is the Divine Word *par excellence,* Muslims consider it inconceivable to "translate" it into any language. A translation is only an explanation of the book's meaning, one interpretation among others. That is why a modern English translation is called "The Meaning of the Glorious Koran": it strives only to give the meaning, but falls short, as any translation must, of reproducing the form of the Holy Book.

According to Islamic doctrine, the style of the Koran is inimitable and of superhuman beauty and power. Not only does the text contain solutions for all problems that arise in the world, but there are also unknown Divine mysteries hidden in the sequence of its verses and in the arrangements of its very letters.

As there is not and cannot be a truly congenial translation of the Koran in any western language, it appears difficult for the untutored reader to understand why millions and millions of Muslims are so absolutely convinced of the greatness and importance of this book, which is usually mentioned with epithets like "noble," "glorious," "pure." What is it that so deeply moves the Muslim when reciting from the Koran, when seeing its verses, or when barely touching it? Goethe says in his *Noten und Abhandlungen:* "The style of the Koran is, in tune with its contents and goal, grand, awesome, and in some places truly sublime."

This judgment is particularly true for the oldest texts of the revelation. One difficulty for the non-Muslim reader—besides the lack of a good translation—is the fact that the present order of the text is not chronological. When the sacred texts were put together in the days of the caliph ʿUthman, the chapters (or *suras*) were arranged in descending length. Thus the first, short revelations—often threats concerning the impending Day of Judgment—are situated at the end of the Koran. Only one brief prayer was chosen as a kind of introduction—the *Fātiḥa,* "the Opening," which roughly corresponds in use to the Lord's Prayer in Christianity, though is probably more frequently recited:

> Praise belongs to God, the Lord of the worlds,
> the Merciful, the Compassionate,
> the Lord at the Day of Judgment.
> Thee we worship and Thee we ask for help.

Guide us on the straight path,
the path of those to whom Thou showest kindness,
not those upon whom Thy wrath rests, nor those who go
astray.

Sura 112 contains the profession of God's unity and is
followed by two brief prayer formulas imploring protection
from evil in various forms. The 114 suras have brief titles
(The Cow, The Star, The Running Ones, etc.), which are
not, however, part of the original sura; they are usually
based on a prominent expression in the text. Groups of inexplicable letters (*ḥā-mīm, ṭā-sīn* and others) precede a
number of suras. Before the recitation of any sura and of
even a single verse, one should utter the formula of protection against the accursed Satan and the *basmala.* The latter
formula is *bismiʾllāhiʾr-raḥmāniʾr-raḥīm,* "In the name of
God, the Merciful, the Compassionate." It precedes all
suras with the exception of Sura 9. Thus, *bismillāh karnā*
means, in Urdu, simply "to begin." In the same way one
says in Turkish, *hadi bismillah,* "Let's start!" The *Fātiḥa*
and a number of short suras are recited during the daily
prayers. Certain suras are thought to possess special blessing power, *baraka;* thus, Sura 36, *Yāsīn,* is usually recited
for dying or dead people. Specific verses are used for the
decoration of buildings, artistically penned tablets, or tal-
ismans. The most famous among these verses is the so-
called Throne Verse (Sura 2/255), which can be found on
walls and weapons, on fabrics and tiles, on agate bezels
and woven in wall hangings because of its beauty and protecting power:

God—there is no god but He, the Living, the Self-
subsistent. Slumber seizeth Him not, neither sleep. To Him
belongeth whatsoever is in the Heavens and whatsoever is
in the Earth. Who is there that shall intercede with Him
save by His Will? He knoweth what is present with men and
what shall befall them, and nought of His knowledge do
they comprehend, save what He willeth. His Throne is as
wide as the Heavens and the Earth, and the keeping of them
wearieth Him not. And He is the High, the Mighty One.

Each single verse of the Koran is called *āyat,* "sign," "miracle" because Muhammad brought forth these verses as Divine signs when his adversaries asked him for a miracle attesting to his prophethood. A few verses were abrogated by later revelations (thus the orders concerning the use of wine); nevertheless they are preserved in the text. This leads, in certain instances, to seeming contradictions which the commentators had to solve.

In the Koran, the position of human beings is described, or rather, alluded to, several times. On the one hand, man is superior to all spirits and angels, for God breathed into Adam "from His breath" (Sura 15/29; 38/72) and ordered the angels to prostrate themselves before Adam whom he wanted to place as a vicegerent, *khalīfa,* on earth. Satan was cursed, having refused to prostrate himself and having claimed "I am better than he" (since he was made from fire, and Adam only from clay). Man's first sin, induced by his eating a certain grain, was not contagious, contrary to the Christian doctrine of original sin, nor was Eve alone the responsible seductress. Human beings are good by nature and change due to the influence of their environment. The absolute bond between man and God is symbolized in the beautiful words of Sura 7/171: before the world was created God drew mankind for a moment from the loins of Adam and asked them, *Alastu bi-rabbikum,* "Am I not your Lord?" They said, "Yes, we testify to it." By this answer the entire human race has expressed its willingness to obey God's orders and has accepted all His decrees in advance; thus they cannot claim ignorance of His commands at the Day of Judgment. This Koranic statement—though interpreted somewhat differently in certain schools—was to become a favorite theme for mystical meditations and poetry. "God has honored the children of Adam" (Sura 17/70); even more, it was humans to whom He gave the *amāna* or "trust", which He had also offered to heaven and earth, but they refused to accept it. Man, despite his ignorance and weakness, accepted the *amāna* (Sura 33/72). The scholars are not in agreement as to what this "trust" may be—is it obedience, faith, responsibility, love, individuality, or the indestructible core of the soul? Human beings are called to ponder when looking at the signs which God has placed "in the horizons [i.e., the world] and in themselves" (Sura 41/53). This means to observe history and nature; one's own heart and soul can lead the way to a deeper religious understanding. Warnings and lessons from history and from nature may help reveal the right path; such insights can be applied to one's own life.

The Koran, which contains in its later suras, especially those revealed in Medina, quite a number of regulations for worldly affairs, daily life, and political order, has been for centuries, and still is, the center and basis of virtually all branches of Islamic learning. The Muslims' preoccupation with its sublime language grew into the study of grammar and rhetoric, especially when non-Arabs entered the fold of Islam in increasing numbers and had to be taught about the peculiarities of the language of revelation. The belief that the Book was untranslatable forced those who embraced Islam to learn Arabic or at least to become acquainted with the Arabic alphabet. This had immense consequences for Persian and Turkish, as well as for the Islamic languages of India, Central Asia, and Africa, and for their literatures. Koranic sayings and expressions are used as much in high literature as in daily conversations even among non-Arabs, but the non-Muslim often misses the subtle allusions.

The Muslims' desire was to recite the Koran as beautifully as possible, and the art of *tilāwat*, the proper musical recitation, developed into a high art. Even when reciting the Book without embellishment, one has to observe certain subtle changes in pronunciation. Generally, however, the Koran is chanted in melodic phrases, somewhat reminiscent of Gregorian chant. The *ḥāfiz*, who "preserves" the Koran, i.e., knows it by heart, is highly respected, and boys (and girls) with beautiful voices are sent at an early age to the mosque to memorize the Book. In order to make the sacred character of the Koran visible, it is wrapped beautifully and hung from the ceiling or any other high place, or it is placed on the uppermost shelf of the bookcase, lest any other book be above it.

Five main religious duties are incumbent upon believers. These are the so-called "pillars of Islam." The first one, the profession of faith, *shahāda,* is basically the foundation of the others. Whoever confesses in public: "I testify that there is no deity save God and that Muhammad is the messenger of God" (*ashhadu an lā ilāha illā'Llāh Muḥammad rasūl Allāh*) has accepted Islam. The *shahāda* is not found exactly in this form in the Koran, but this does sum up Islam's central points. In the course of the first centuries, when foreign influences and currents increasingly surrounded Islam, a more extensive creed was developed with the aim of defining exactly Islam's position. This creed states, in keeping with various Koranic verses, that the believer has to accept all the prophets who taught before Muhammad, while Muhammad is the last messenger, who brought the concluding revelation which corrects the previous ones.

The Koran calls Muhammad "a human being like you to whom revelation was brought," but as a result of various Koranic allusions to miraculous events, a long garland of legends soon surrounded him. (The two most important events are his nightly journey to Jerusalem and then into the presence of God, Sura 17/1; and the 'splitting of the moon', Sura 54/1). Many other miracles were ascribed to him too, and in the course of time he reached, in theology, the status of the Perfect Man, *al-insān al-kāmil,* and was considered the meaning and end of creation. This idea was expressed best in the extra-Koranic Divine word *laulāka laulāka mā khalaqtu'l-aflāka,* "If you had not been (i.e., but for your sake) I would not have created the spheres." Muslims have always emphasized that it is, correctly speaking, the second half of the profession of faith by which Islam defines itself as an independent religion: many people will confess God's unity and unicity, but the practical aspects are brought by Muhammad; to obey the laws he preached means to follow God's will as it is revealed in the divine Book.

Besides the profession of faith, the pillars of Islam are the ritual prayer, the alms tax, fasting in Ramadan, and the pilgrimage to Mecca. The so-called Holy War, *jihād* (literally "striving, exertion" in the way of God) was never made a pillar. Prayer will be dealt with in detail on pp. 39–42. The third pillar is *zakāt,* the alms tax. As its root *zky* shows, it was meant originally as self-purification and considered as a "loan to God." The law regulated exactly the payable amount; the income should be used, according to Sura 9/60, for the poor, the needy, the tax collector; for those whose religious zeal needs to be strengthened; for slaves who want to buy themselves out of slavery; for debtors who by financing good works have become impoverished; and finally *fī sabīl Allāh,* "in the way of God," that is, for different purposes such as helping needy travelers, or building useful structures such as public fountains. *Zakāt* is also used, as recently in Pakistan, to found religious schools. *Zakāt,* correctly applied, appears to be a protective measure against both capitalism and communism, provided it is distributed by taxing the wealthy and supporting the needy. This is the opinion not only of modern Muslim thinkers (e.g., Iqbal, d. 1938), but also of Christian scholars such as Louis Massignon and Kenneth Cragg.

It seems that today fasting is the most strictly observed duty, although it may appear to outsiders to be the most demanding one. During the whole month of Ramadan, the ninth month of the Islamic lunar year (which consists of 354 days), the Muslim is not allowed to eat, drink, smoke, smell perfume, have intercourse, or even have an injection during the daytime. This injunction begins at early dawn when it is light enough to discern a black thread from a white one, and lasts to the completion of sunset. Every morning one has to formulate anew the intention, *niyya,* to keep the fast. Travelers, senior citizens, pregnant and nursing women, as well as ailing people, need not keep the fast but have to make up for the lost days at some other time or to make compensation for each day by such actions as feeding the poor. Some modernists, like the late-President Bourghiba, have attempted to declare agricultural and industrial work as a "minor *jihād*" against hunger and poverty in order to relieve the working population from such a hard duty—because in wartime one need not keep the fast.

Due to the lunar calendar the month of Ramadan wanders through all seasons. It is hardest in summer when one is not permitted even a drop of water during the heat. Likewise, Muslims living in northern areas suffer great hardship due to the long days in the northern summers when the sun remains visible for eighteen or twenty hours and more. In this case, according to some legal opinions, the Muslim may accept as the end of the day the moment of sunset in the closest Muslim country—that would be Turkey for most of Europe, or North Africa for Mediterranean countries.

After breaking the fast with some water, and ideally an odd number of dates, the evening prayer is performed, and after the fast-breaking dinner, *ifṭār*, a series of twenty or thirty-three or more prayer cycles (*rakʿa*) is performed by the pious (this is called the *tarāwīḥ* prayer). In previous times the nights of Ramadan were celebrated with much merrymaking. Just before dawn one usually eats a light meal. In Turkey many of those who are not regular at their daily prayers still keep the fast or strive to fast at least a few days, especially on the days preceding the *lailat al-qadr*, the night when the first revelation of the Koran took place (see Sura 97). It is celebrated on one of the last odd nights in Ramadan, usually on the 27th. The belief is that the whole world is filled with light during this night, when the Divine Word had manifested itself to humankind. Some people spend the last ten days of the month in seclusion in the mosque to partake of the spiritual blessings of Ramadan. The appearance of the new moon is expected with great anticipation, as it means the end of fasting. At the *ʿīd ul-fiṭr*, the Feast of Fastbreaking, cities are lavishly decorated, new garments are worn, and gifts are exchanged and distributed (hence the Turkish expression *sheker bayrami*, "sugar feast.") The month of fasting, hard as it appears to a non-Muslim, is a time of rejoicing in many Muslim countries because those who perform it feel united with millions of other believers who, by "taming their lower souls" strive for purification. In the pilgrimage to Mecca, the *ḥajj*, ancient Arab rites have been taken over and spiritualized. The pilgrimage is performed during the last lunar month, Dhu'l-hijja. People who come to Arabia at other times can perform the lesser pilgrimage, *ʿumra*, which consists mainly of the circumambulation of the Kaʿba and the running between two hillocks called Safa and Marwa.

Pilgrimage to a sacred place requires a ritual consecration. Thus, at a certain distance from Mecca the men, with shaven heads, put on a special garment, *iḥrām*, consisting of two white unsewn pieces of cloth that cover their whole body; women put on a covering garment. Pilgrims greet the sacred precincts with the call *labbaika*, "Here I am at Thy service!" The rites that have to be performed include the sevenfold circumambulation of the Kaʿba (where one tries to kiss the black stone in its southeastern corner) and a sevenfold running between Safa and Marwa, which are now connected by covered arcades. But the central rite is the "staying" on the hill ʿArafat, a distance of some eight miles from Mecca, on the ninth day of the month. There, sermons are given, and on the way back the 'stoning of Satan' is performed by casting seven pebbles three times at a certain place. After that, on the tenth day of the month, each pilgrim slaughters a sheep or larger animal in Mina. Those staying home do the same. This part of the ritual commemorates the day when Abraham was ordered to sacrifice his son Ismaʿil, whose place was then taken by a ram. After the Feast of Offering the pilgrim can return from the sacred state, *iḥrām*, into the normal state, when the cutting of hair and nails, as well as sex, are again permitted. Killing any creatures inside the sacred area is considered a major sin.

The pilgrimage should be performed only when the pilgrim is in good health and can undertake the journey without major difficulties, especially without incurring debts; this shows the realistic approach of Islam to religious practice. In former centuries the pilgrimage was a dangerous undertaking for those who came from distant lands, whether they traveled overland in the caravans which started, with great pomp, in Cairo or Baghdad, or sailed from India or Malaysia on fragile boats. (Air travel is not always very safe either.) Yet modern Muslims sometimes express the view that these slow, arduous journeys prepared them better for the great event than the brief trip by air, which barely leaves leisure to meditate on the experience of visiting the center of their religion. On their return the pilgrims bring a vessel filled with wholesome water from the well Zamzam, from which Hagar once drank. They are received by their families with pride and joy, and are called Hajji. Those who die during the pilgrimage are regarded as martyrs, *shahīd*, "witness" for their faith.

Doubtlessly the meeting of people from all parts of the world in Mecca and their common worship at the central sanctuary of Islam does much to strengthen the feeling of unity among Muslims. Through the centuries many scholars and pious people extended their stay in Mecca and exchanged their religious views with colleagues from other parts of the world. The sojourn near the Kaʿba inspired important theological and mystical works: the comprehensive commentary on the Koran by Zamakhshari (called by the honorific title *Jār Allah*, "God's neighbor" due to his prolonged stay in Mecca) grew out of the author's stay in Mecca. Even more evident is the influence of the Meccan experience on the most comprehensive work of Islamic theosophy, the *Futūḥāt al-makkiyya*, of Ibn ʿArabi, which was "revealed" to the author while he was circumambulating the Kaʿba.

Furthermore, it is important to remember that almost all reform movements in the fringe areas of the Islamic world were triggered off by the pilgrimage. Faithful believers from Bengal and Nigeria, from Morocco and Central Asia, who had lived for some time in Mecca and exchanged their views with others who, like them, had experienced what seemed to be the 'true Arabic Islam', returned to their countries to fight the numerous indigenous superstitions and customs which had infiltrated the Islam of the masses and which now appeared to them like remnants of ancient paganism.

It became customary, though not obligatory, to combine a visit to Mecca with a visit to the Prophet's mausoleum, *rauḍa,* in Medina, and many are the poems from at least the late thirteenth century in which Muslims in distant areas such as India, Indonesia, or sub-saharan Africa expressed their longing for the last resting place of their beloved Prophet.

The duty that seems most important for the Muslim's daily life and which has shaped the Islamic world most strongly is the second pillar, ritual prayer, *ṣalāt* (in Persian and Turkish, *namāz*). It has been said that "between faith and unbelief lies the giving up of ritual prayers." The *ṣalāt* is performed five times in twenty-four hours: the hour before sunrise, noon, afternoon, after sunset, and nightfall. The Koran does not mention the number of obligatory prayers, but five prayers seem to have been customary in Muhammad's lifetime. The number was fixed, as the hadith literature tells us, when Muhammad was pleading with God about the duties of the faithful during his nocturnal journey to heaven. The Koran emphasizes the nightly prayer, *tahajjud,* which, however, was never made a binding duty for believers, but was and still is practiced among the pious and in particular among mystics.

Every prayer begins with the *niyya,* the formulation of the intention, for instance, to perform the evening prayer with its three cycles or *rakʿa.* During one *rakʿa* the praying person stands upright, uttering the words *Allāhu akbar,* "God is greater [than anything else]" and the Fātiḥa. Then one bends from the hips, straightens one's posture, prostrates, sits, and then performs another prostration. In the first two *rakʿa,* another chapter or some verses from the Koran are also recited. Each prayer consists of a prescribed number of *rakʿa* (daybreak prayer, two; noon, four; afternoon, four; sunset, three; and night prayer, four). The various movements and positions are accompanied by special

formulae. At the prayer's end one utters the profession of
faith while sitting, as well as a formula of blessings on the
Prophet and the believers.

The *ṣalāt* can be extended by reciting long parts of the
Koran in the first two *rakʿa;* many people also add a lengthy
meditation while using the rosary, *tasbīḥ,* repeating religious formulas or Divine Names and invocations. Besides
the five required *ṣalāt* there are many recommended *ṣalāts*
that can also be performed throughout the day.

When prayer time begins, the muezzin calls from the
minaret of the mosque or, in some areas, from its roof. The
call to prayer, *adhān,* consists of the profession of faith and
some additional short phrases and is sung in long cadences.
Nowadays this is usually done with the help of loudspeakers
or from tapes. Once the *adhān* is over, the believer under-
takes the ablution. He or she can perform the prayer alone
in any clean place or else in the mosque with the community; in both cases absolute ritual purity is the first condi-
tion. After each minor pollution (caused by solid, liquid, or
gaseous matters leaving the lower part of the body, as well
as sleep or fainting), the minor ablution, *wuḍūʾ,* is required:
the face, part of the head, the arms to the elbows, the feet
to the ankles have to be washed in running water that has
not been touched by anyone. The details of the ablutions,
elaborated exactly in the course of time, have to be observed minutely, from the intaking of the water in the nos-
trils to the movement of the fingers when cleansing the
ears; each movement should be accompanied by a specific
prayer formula. If none of the above-mentioned pollutions
occurred between two prayers, one need not perform the
ablution. After major pollutions such as sex, menstruation,
and childbirth, a full bath, *ghusl,* is required in which no
place in the whole body, including the hair, can remain dry.
Only then may the prayer be performed and the Koran
touched and recited. It is a pious custom to perform *ghusl*
before the communal prayer on Friday noon, even though
no major pollution exists. In case water cannot be found,
one may perform the ablution with sand (*tayammum*).

The Friday prayer is a duty of the community; it contains a short sermon, *khutba*, which consists of two parts. It gives some advice usually based on the Koran or the *hadīth*, and a prayer for the ruler of the government. To be mentioned in the *khutba* meant to be the legitimate ruler. Women rarely attend the Friday prayer but prefer to pray at home. The daily prayers are explained in the Koran as acts of humility and adoration. At the end of the prayer the Muslim can mention his/her personal requests. While traveling or in war or under duress, one can perform the noon and afternoon or sunset and night prayers together. One also has numerous opportunities to perform additional prayers of two or more *rakʿa* each, e.g., during solar or lunar eclipses; when performing the rain prayer; when entering or leaving the house or the mosque—in short, some pious Muslims use every opportunity to perform a brief *salāt*.

The belief in the purifying power of ritual prayer is intense; the Prophet compared it to a stream of water that washes off sins five times a day. The performance of the prayer at the prescribed time constitutes ideally a means of educating Muslims to punctuality, cleanliness, and, since there is no ranking in the mosque, equal participation in the life of the community. Prayer can also lead to ecstatic experiences, and when one observes a praying Muslim who is oblivious of everything around him and seems to have drawn himself, as it were, out of this world to stand humbly before the Lord, one realizes best whence Islam derives its vital strength.

To perform the *salāt*, a clean spot suffices, be it in the fields, in the train, or in one's shop or office. A small prayer rug guarantees the cleanliness of the place. However, even in the Prophet's lifetime a place for congregational worship was established, called *masjid*, "the place where one prostrates" (hence the word *Mosque*). The great mosque, where the Friday prayer is held and which was found in each quarter, is called *jāmiʿ*, "the gathering [mosque]." Mainly in the eastern part of the Islamic world, one finds small open prayer places called *muṣallā*, and for the gathering of large congregations at the two *ʿīd*, the end of Ramadan and the Feast of Offerings, one sometimes uses an *ʿidgāh*, a vast enclosure with a prayer niche.

The architecture of the mosque can be considered the best known and, to a certain degree, most representative artistic expression of Islamic culture. The great mosque of Samarra, the temporary residence of the Abbasid caliphs in the ninth century, provides a classical example of early mosque architecture; its twenty-five naves offer space enough for a hundred thousand people to pray. Even better known is the great mosque in Cordova (929) with its forest-like array of large columns connected by simple and double horseshoe arches. Under the influence of and often in conjunction with the theological college, *madrasah*, which developed first in the east, the pillared courtyards of the large early mosques were later replaced by vast courtyards surrounded by deep niches and porticoes; the facades became larger and more monumental; immense gates, often decorated with stalactite work, are typical in particular of the Turkish-Persian areas, including Mamluk Egypt and parts of Muslim India. Yet the most perfect architectural form of the mosque seems to be represented by the Ottoman type with its enormous central dome. It developed, as it were, in competition with the Byzantine Hagia Sophia in Istanbul after two- and multi-domed mosques had prevailed in the Turkish areas. The most superb examples of this style were reached in Mimar Sinan's imperial mosques in Istanbul and Edirne (Süleymaniye, Selimiye, Mihrimah). The central dome, which grows out of the cubic building and a number of half domes, contrasts with the slim, high minarets; this style has shaped the western image of how a mosque should look.

The shapes of the minarets are as different as those of the mosques. The old Syrian and western Islamic type—rectangular and rather heavy towers—still exist in Morocco and Spain (the Giralda in Seville); the spiral minaret of Samarra (built in 850) with its height of more than 150 feet is reminiscent of the Babylonian ziggurat. Late medieval

Egypt's many-storeyed Mamluk minarets, often heavily ornamented, contrast with the simple forms used generally in Iran and Central Asia, which are somehow similar to high round chimneys and are often decorated with fine brick or tile mosaic. The Ottoman needle-shaped minaret is quite different from the somewhat heavier forms in the Indian subcontinent, which are usually crowned by pavillion-like structures or, in the Deccan, resemble little flower bulbs at their tip, just as the domes of the Deccani mosques sometimes seem to grow out of petals. There are numerous regional forms of both mosques and minarets in Indonesia and in China, where a pagoda type is prevalent; and simple but impressive forms appear in West Africa.

A special area for women, either in the background or on a gallery, is usually included in the mosque.

The furnishing of the mosque is extremely simple. In the courtyard one finds a well, a fountain, or a basin for the ablutions. The direction to Mecca is indicated by a small niche, *miḥrāb,* in the wall. The *miḥrāb* can consist of any clean material: wood, tile work (especially in the rather flat, angular Seljukid *miḥrābs*), luster tiles, stone, or marble. It is usually surrounded by artistically written verses from the Koran, in particular the saying from Sura 3/32: "Whenever Zakariya entered the *miḥrāb* . . . ," a sentence that points to the young virgin Mary's being miraculously sustained in her special room. The exact orientation of the *miḥrāb* toward the Kaʿba was an important problem for architects and mathematicians.

Among the *miḥrābs* in the Muslim world, two deserve special mention. One is located in the mosque of Bijapur, Deccan, and was built in 1636. Measuring some 18 to 21 feet, it is probably the largest *miḥrāb* ever built. It is decorated with inscriptions in à-jour work with innumerable colorful and golden decorative details; stone "curtains" over niches in the lower corners remind the viewer of baroque architecture (Portuguese influence cannot be excluded in this area). The other remarkable prayer niche was inaugurated in 1988 in the Faisal Mosque in Islamabad, Pakistan; it has the shape of an open book, made of white marble on whose pages Sura 55, *Ar-Raḥmān,* "The All Merciful," is engraved in golden calligraphy in a medieval style. Often, the motif of the niche appears on prayer rugs, especially those from Iran and Turkey; this motif has been used for centuries, sometimes with the addition of a lamp or of ewers, which may point to the vessels used for ablution or the symbolism of light and purifying water.

Besides the prayer niche stands the *minbar,* a pulpit which was introduced in the days of the Prophet. It consisted originally of three steps, but later a greater number of steps are found. The *minbar,* like the *miḥrāb,* can be made of any material; the finest examples are those of wood carved in complicated geometrical and vegetabilian designs.

A stand for the Koran, usually of fine woodwork and often with precious inlay of ivory or mother-of-pearl, is positioned close to the *miḥrāb;* glass lamps, in former times decorated with shimmering enamel inscriptions, illuminate the mosque. A (rather modern) clock shows the time of prayer, and in large congregational mosques in a state capital a special place for the rulers, e.g., a pavillion-like structure, may be erected.

There is no pictorial decoration on the walls; only writing and sometimes endless arabesque motifs serve for decorative purposes. Tile work in geometrical shapes with invocations of the names of God and His messenger (in Shia Islam also that of ʿAli, the first *imām*) are used from the later Middle Ages. Star tiles with scribbled verses from the Koran were typical of thirteenth-century Iran. The tile work of Ottoman mosques, especially that of Rüstem Pasha's small mosque in Istanbul with its thousands of tulip motifs, is fascinating. Wall painting, generally arabesques or, somewhat later, flower motifs appear in pre-modern times. Nowadays one can sometimes find in mosques a picture of the Kaʿba in Mecca, or of the Prophet's mausoleum in Medina, or even a representation of the Prophet's blessed sandal.

Scriptural decoration, however, is most frequent, for calligraphy is the Islamic art par excellence: through letters the sacred word of God has become visible, and copies of the Scripture are handed over from generation to generation even though oral recitation has always been and still is considered more important than the written word. From the earliest times Muslims strove to write copies of the Koran as beautifully as possible. The oldest and somewhat ungainly form of Arabic writing, i.e., the stiff ductus, whose more developed form was called *Kufic* (from the city of Kufa), was not very practical: it lacked diacritical marks, and a number of letters could not be distinguished properly. But these early manuscripts were probably intended for those who had memorized the Koran and who now and then might need some visual help.

Somewhat later, diacritical marks and vowel signs were added. The letters, heavy and stately, were written in vellum codices in broad format, and the page invites the reader or onlooker to contemplate the text almost like an icon. Slowly the script became lighter and more elegant. It was used not only in precious manuscripts but even more importantly in epigraphy (tombstones, historical inscriptions, religious texts). The letters were often placed on an intricate floral background or else shaped into complicated designs with the high letters ending in palmettes or knotted into sophisticated geometrical forms, so that the difference between script and ornament was almost lost. (This is valid in epigraphy; texts in books had always to remain legible.) Besides the Kufic, only used for sacred or very important texts, a cursive script developed, first on papyrus; it was used for profane texts such as letters and non-religious books. Once the Arabs learned the art of paper-making from the Chinese in 751, the script could be shaped according to aesthetic rules. At the beginning of the tenth century the Baghdadian minister Ibn Muqla invented an exact geometrical measuring system for the letters, the breadth of the reed pen being the yardstick for the format of each letter. The various cursive styles were constantly refined and reached a highpoint with classical Ottoman calligraphy. Besides the upright ductus, which was particularly fitting for Arabic, a so-called ''hanging'' style, more in tune with the grammatical exigencies of Persian, developed in Iran. It became the ideal vehicle for poetical texts in Persian, Turkish, and Urdu, but not for Arabic; hence only very few copies of the Koran were penned in this so-called *nasta῾līq*.

To write a copy of the Koran or at least some of its verses was the goal of many educated Muslims, including the rulers, and a good many copies of the Koran and decorative inscriptions with Koranic invocations are the work of Muslim kings, whether in Tunisia or India, in Turkey or Egypt.

The artistic possibilities of the Arabic script are inexhaustible, beginning with large lines that impress the reader by their seeming simplicity (the largest-known copy of the Koran measures 101 to 177 centimeters, with seven lines on the page). In artificial calligrams, religious formulas or invocations appear in animal or vegetable form and even in the shape of faces. Such calligrams, however, are never used for the Koran, since pictorial illumination of the Koran is out of the question. To be sure, the Koran itself does not explicitly prohibit pictorial representation; remarks pertaining to pictures and sculptures are found in the sayings of the Prophet. Wall painting is attested from Umayyad times, and figurative elements on ceramics and metalwork form an important part of Islamic art. Yet this art found its best expression in calligraphy and ornaments. The arabesque, that is, strictly speaking, a tendril that grows through leaves, palmettes, and flowers without end, ever expanding, is the central motif of Islamic art. The decorative pattern of the—seemingly—central motif continues infinitely by being doubled, halved, or by means of simple or twisted mirror effects, all based on sophisticated mathematical rules. Thus the design draws the eye upward and makes the meditating spirit remember the infinite and inexhaustible power of God. Along with calligraphy (which again is transformed into ornament) and which translates and announces God's word, the arabesque is a suitable ornament for both the Sacred Book and the sacred space.

In a very few old miniatures, portraits of the Prophet are found; usually he is shown, if at all, with his face veiled. Again, script takes the role of the picture: the Arabic description of the Prophet's beautiful form and qualities, preserved in the most ancient traditions, is often written in fine lettering and used instead of a picture in many Muslim houses. Lately, however, pictures of the Koranic prophets and of the Shia *imāms* appear in Shia Iran, and primitive representations of the Buraq, on which the Prophet performed his nightly journey, can be acquired in Indian and Pakistani mosques and decorate Pakistani trucks as a kind of protective symbol.

The Koran is the basis for the entire life, be it the regulation of religious duties or problems of art. Hence it is natural that a vast range of interpretations and commentaries should have developed in the course of the centuries. The first step in the interpretation of the Koran was philological scrutiny of the text. Although the Koran is considered to be God's uncreated word, in the very first period some minor variants existed which were of minimal importance; to this day one speaks of the "seven ways of reciting" the holy Book although, thanks to the printing press, a near uniformity has now been achieved.

In the first generations after Muhammad most of the pious refused to interpret the Koran: they were afraid lest they be led into dangerous aberrations and speculations by introducing legendary material. But there has never been a completely uniform exegesis. Rather, the possibility of interpreting the Book in the most diverse ways seems to be a strong proof of its supernatural origin. As God's word it has to be as infinite as He Himself, and thus its different possibilities have never ceased to occupy the minds of scholars, mystics, and simple believers. The first major commentary, comprising not less than thirty volumes, was written by Tabari, the famed historian (d. 935). Zamakhshari (d. 1146) composed his famous commentary under the influence of Mu'tazilite ideas, but the somewhat sectarian attitude was generally overlooked due to the author's excellent philological exegesis. Among the famous later commentaries one should mention Baidawi in the thirteenth century, and Jalaluddin as-Suyuti in the late fifteenth, while in Ottoman Turkey in the nineteenth century

Elmali's commentary is often used. Through translations, which are in themselves a kind of commentary, scholars in the non-Arab countries have tried to rescue the sacred text from the numberless layers of commentaries and metacommentaries that had almost completely covered the text; they tried to lead Muslims back to the exact wording and meaning of the revelation instead of dwelling upon this or that scholar's glosses. The Persian translation of the Koran by the Indian theologian Shah Waliullah (d. 1762) is a major step in this direction.

Needless to say, the mystics of Islam have striven to reach a more profound understanding of the Divine word. They knew that a deeper meaning lies behind the words of the text and that one has to penetrate to the true core. It may be an exaggeration that an early mystic supposedly knew 7,000 interpretations for each verse of the Koran, but the search for the never-ending meanings of the Koran has continued through the ages. The Arabic language has been very helpful in this respect with its almost infinite possibilities of developing the roots of words and forming cross-relations between expressions. A classical example is the work of Ibn ʿArabi, which is fully (or at least mainly) understandable only on the basis of the Koran and its interpretation. Shiite groups in Islam, especially the Batiniyya, always stressed the esoteric meaning of the Koranic word and introduced their followers into this sacred and secret area through a step-by-step initiation. Does not the inner meaning of the word correspond to the spirit which gives life to the exoteric body of the words? Is not the Koran a double-sided brocade whose exterior and interior are equally beautiful but attract different kinds of people, as Maulana Rumi says?

But whoever has studied the Koran admits that reading and reciting it is a veritable conversation with God, who can be approached only through His word. Therefore one would be justified in calling the reading of the Koran a "sacrament".

In the Middle ages, a kind of cabalistic interpretation developed (*wifq, jafr*) and even in our time certain sects and groups among the Muslims try to find the deeper meaning of the number of letters on each page, their numerical value, and their combinations. They do so overlooking the fact that the copies they use belong to a rather late arrangement and that their format differs from that of the early and medieval pages.

Developments in modern times have challenged many religious positions, and representatives of both scholarship and piety are looking for a new understanding of the Koran. Since it is considered valid for all times as the final revelation, it must contain all the scientific discoveries of the modern age. The former rector of the al-Azhar university in Cairo, Mustafa al-Maraghi, said in this respect:

> True religion cannot conflict with truth, and when we are positively convinced of the truth of any scientific remark which seems to be incompatible with Islam, this is only because we do not understand correctly the Koran and the traditions. In our religion we possess a universal teaching which declares that, when an apodictic truth contradicts a revealed text, we have to interpret the text allegorically.

Before him, the Indian reformer Sir Sayyid Ahmad Khan (d. 1898) had mentioned in his writings that "the work of God," that is, God's work as visible in nature, cannot contradict the "Word of God," as revealed in the Koran. (The terms are given in English in the Urdu text.)

Interpreters in the late nineteenth and twentieth centuries sometimes try to find references in the Koran to prove scientific discoveries, social and military inventions up to the hydrogen bomb, or to interpret certain remarks as referring to modern events. The eschatological suras have often been divested of their original meaning and interpreted as predictions about the development of humanity, unless they are understood as pointing to the destruction of our world by human folly and the use of nuclear weapons. One can indeed speak of a demythologization of the Koran, and lately its legalistic aspects have been highlighted in most "fundamentalist" circles, as the Law is considered to be the "spiritual regulator" of the community. Nevertheless, the Indo-Muslim modernist Muhammad Iqbal has constantly repeated that the Koran is the expression of a dynamic, "anti-classical" spirit, full of life, and not a textbook of natural sciences, and that the "world of the Koran" reveals a new face every day, without end—for when God is infinite so also is His word as revealed in His Book.

The Tradition

At an early moment in their history Muslims discovered
that the Koran does not sufficiently explain all the details in
the individual's or the community's life: many problems are
mentioned only in passing; others are not mentioned at all.
As the revelation stopped for good with the Prophet's
death, another way to organize life according to the Divine
commands had to be found. Muhammad's companions and
the first generations after him looked for a way to fill the
gaps while remaining faithful to the spirit of the revelation.
They therefore clung to the Prophet's own words and actions, his *sunna,* "custom." Already in pre-Islamic Arabia,
tradition was valued very highly, and as the Bedouin strove
to follow his venerated ancestors' or elders' way of life
closely, so also, after the advent of Islam, believers tried to
imitate their beloved Prophet's example in each and every
detail. Did not the Koran itself state: "Verily in the messenger of God you have a beautiful model for everyone who
hopes for God and the Last Judgment and often remembers
God" (Sura 33/21)?

The Prophet's custom, his *sunna,* thus became in itself a kind of interpretation of the Koran. Certain allusions, as well as facts that were only vaguely mentioned or indicated in the Scripture, had to be understood as Muhammad had shown by his words and his actions. His words were collected and his actions told and retold from generation to generation; a single report of what he said or did is called a *ḥadīth,* "saying, tale." As in every oral tradition, a good number of non-authentic sayings infiltrated the text in the course of the first centuries. Therefore the *ḥadīth* can not be considered an absolutely infallible source for our understanding of Muhammad's original teachings and his actual behavior. They also reflect, at least to a certain extent, the different currents developing inside Islam, for theological and political factions came up with *ḥadīth* that supported their ideals. In the ninth century tens of thousands of *ḥadīth* were in circulation, and it was the great achievement of Bukhari (d. 870) to have selected and classified the most reliable ones in his comprehensive collection, which contains some 7,300 *ḥadīth,* many of which, however, appear under different headings, so that the total number is near 3,000. Bukhari's contemporary, Muslim (d. 875), undertook a similar task. The collections produced by these two scholars are called *ṣaḥīḥ,* "sound, without flaw," and they are regarded as second only to the Koran. The four other collections that were produced at about the same time (by Abu Daʾud, Nasaʾi, Tirmidhi, and Ibn Maja) rank somewhat lower. Scholars traveled widely in search of reliable *ḥadīth,* for *ḥadīth* criticism is based upon specific criteria, which may look somewhat strange to a western scholar. Each *ḥadīth* consists of the text, *matn,* and the *isnād,* the chain of those who have heard the text in question. This chain has to continue without interruption to Muhammad or one of his companions. A typical short *isnād* would look something like this: "I heard from A that he said: 'I heard from B that he was told by C that his father said: "I heard the Prophet say . . . " '." The duty of those who study *ḥadīth* is primarily to test the reliability of the traditionist. One has to find out whether or not a person mentioned in the *isnād* (among whom are a considerable number of women) really knew the one from whom he relates the *ḥadīth*, or whether time, age, and local distance make their relation improbable if not impossible. There are several more criteria as well. Out of this scrutiny a whole branch of scholarship developed, that of "the men", *ʿilm ur-rijāl*, i.e., biographies of the transmitters; these were then arranged according to "classes", *ṭabaqāt*, based on temporal distance from the Prophet. If a chain of transmitters fulfilled all the conditions (which also implied that they were honest, pious, and reliable), then the *ḥadīth* was considered to be *ṣaḥīḥ*, "sound"; other, less "sound" *ḥadīth* were "good" or "weak." These careful investigations notwithstanding, new *ḥadīth* apparently found their way into literature: Jewish and Christian adages (thus Matthew 25:37–40), and words of wisdom from classical antiquity appear in Islamicized garb.

A number of extra-Koranic words of God quoted by the Prophet, so-called *ḥadīth qudsī*, "sacred *ḥadīth*" were transmitted among believers and in particular among Sufis.

Contrary to a quotation from the Koran, which is always regarded as God's word, a *ḥadīth* begins with the phrase: "He (or The Prophet), God bless him and give him peace, said." This formula is always used when mentioning the Prophet. The *ḥadīth* itself, as everything connected with the Prophet, is called *sharīf*, "noble."

A "scientific" critique of *ḥadīth* in the western sense is suspect for most pious Muslims, and besides, it is considered irrelevant, as Muhammad, being a true prophet, could have foreseen and foretold many future developments and given much advice which western investigators might see as a foreign import. There are, however, some modernist schools in Islam which reject the authenticity of *ḥadīth*, and reject it in toto. The Indian Muslim, Chiragh Ali (d. 1894), a colleague of the modernist Sir Sayyid Ahmad Khan, attacked *ḥadīth* literature even more sharply than Ignaz Goldziher did at the same time in Europe. His attitude is likely to have strengthened the aversion of the traditionalists and especially the *Ahl-i ḥadīth* (a fundamentalist

movement) against Sir Sayyid's reformist tendencies.
Among contemporary scholars who strictly deny the importance of *ḥadīth* in its entirety as a source for Islamic life and
culture, one must single out Ghulam Ahmad Parvez in Pakistan, for whom the Koran constitutes the one and only
source for Muslim thought; his interpretation of the Sacred
Book is, however, rather idiosyncratic. For him, the Koran
is "the end of religion," as he states with a formula reminiscent of Karl Barth. On the other hand the Pakistani Fazlur Rahman (d. 1988 in Chicago) elaborated the concept of
the "living *sunna*" in order to show Muslims a practicable
way into the future. What mattered for him was not to imitate slavishly whatever Muslims had done more than a
thousand years ago in following the Prophet's example, but
rather to understand the spirit of the *sunna* in the same way
that early believers had: not as a mechanical imitation but
as an attempt to enter into the spirit of the *ḥadīth* and re-
interpret it for modern times.

The traditional style was to strive for a perfect *imitatio
Muhammadi*, to follow the Prophet's example in every detail, be it the position of one's hands during prayer, or the
right way to don a pair of trousers or to wind one's turban—
everything is derived from the Prophet's example. "Muhammad ibn Aslam did not eat melons because there was
no *ḥadīth* how the Prophet used to eat them"—this is a
classical example. But still in the nineteenth-century a pious Indian Muslim refused to eat the favorite fruit of Indians, i.e., mangos, because he was not sure whether or not
the Prophet had enjoyed this fruit, let alone how he might
have eaten it.

The opposite of *sunna*, "custom," is *bidʿa*, "innova-
tion," and it is the introduction of *bidʿas* that was seen as a
great danger for the stability of the community, even though
"good *bidʿas*" were acceptable according to still another
ḥadīth.

The most interesting and far-reaching example of imitation of the Prophet is circumcision, never mentioned in
the Koran: it is called in Turkish simply *sünnet*, i.e., *sunna*.

A number of theologians consider prayer performed by an uncircumcised man valid. However, according to tradition, the Prophet was born circumcised, and for most people circumcision is the distinguishing feature of the Muslim man. The operation, which is performed on boys between the fourth and the tenth years (usually about age seven), is called in Indo-Pakistan *musulmānī*, for by undergoing it the boy becomes a real member of the community. The day is celebrated with great joy, and circumcisions of high-ranking boys such as princes were formerly connected with costly public entertainment.

Female circumcision, based on a barely known *hadīth*, is customary not only in fringe groups in southern Egypt and the Indian border regions, but also in certain sophisticated communities such as the Bohoras.

Again not in the Koran but in tradition, one finds the basis for sacred days or nights. The Prophet's birthday is celebrated on 12 Rabiʿ al-awwal, the third lunar month. This is also, and primarily, the anniversary of the Prophet's death and is therefore celebrated as a mourning day in certain areas. Celebrations of the birthday are mentioned first in Fatimid times, for the Fatimid's ancestress Fatima was the Prophet's daughter, and celebrating his birthday added to the religious and political prestige of the dynasty. A colorful description of a *maulūd*, "birthday," held in Arbela (modern Irbil in northern Iraq) in 1207, shows that illumination and the recitation of special eulogies was already practiced. Soon, the celebrations spread to the Maghrib. Hymnic texts in high-flown prose and simple poetry to be recited on this day were composed in all Islamic languages. One of the most famous works of this genre is Süleyman Chelebi's *Mevlûd-i sherif* from around 1400; it tells in simple Turkish verses the miracles that happened during the Prophet's birth. This *Mevlûd* is not only recited in simple melodies during the birthday proper, but at various religious events, especially at the fortieth day after a bereavement or at the anniversary of a death, for the recitation of this poem, combined with readings from the Koran and prayers, is meritorious and salutory. The entire creation welcomes the newborn savior who is sent "as Mercy for the worlds" (Sura 21/107):

> Welcome, O high prince, we welcome you!
> Welcome, O mine of wisdom, we welcome you!
> Welcome, O secret of the Book, we welcome you!
> Welcome, O medicine for pain, we welcome you!
> Welcome, O sunlight and moonlight from God, we
> welcome you!
> Welcome, O you not separated from God!
> Welcome, O nightingale of the Garden of Beauty!
> Welcome, O friend of the Lord of Power!
> Welcome, O refuge of your community!
> Welcome, O helper of the poor and destitute. . . .
> Welcome, O intercessor for the sinner!
> Only for you were Time and Space created . . .

The same heavenly blessings which the pious Turk hopes for when listening to or reciting this lovely old poem are expected also by Muslims in other areas, whether their *maulūds* are written in Swahili, Bengali, or Sindhi.

The 12 Rabiᶜ al-awwal is, or was in many countries, a public holiday, and the whole month is devoted to recitations of religious texts and sermons over radio or TV (as in Pakistan). But while traditional Islam would sing of the wondrous events during the Prophet's birth, such as the light that shone from his mother or the greetings that birds and beasts offered to the newborn, in modern times the main emphasis has shifted from the miraculous aspects of the Prophet's birth to his role as the leader of his community, the true model of ethical behavior, the social reformer and just leader. To imitate these noble qualities of his seems to many Muslims more important than to follow meticulously the outward aspects of his *sunna*. But one should keep in mind that the *imitatio Muhammadi*, with its attention to all the minute details of daily life, has given the Muslim community all over the world a remarkable uniformity.

One of the celebrations which cannot be derived from the Koran but has become important since the Middle Ages is the *lailat al-barāʾa* or *shab-i barāt* on 15 Shaʿban, the night of the full moon preceding the beginning of Ramadan. On this night, it is believed, sins are forgiven and one's fate for the new year is determined. Mosques are illuminated, fireworks are performed in some areas, and special sweets are distributed. Also important is the night of the Prophet's heavenly journey on the 27 Rajab (seventh lunar month) as well as the first nights of this month (conception of the Prophet).

The Shia tradition celebrates the day of Ghadir Khum, on 17 Dhuʾl-hijja, when the Prophet declared ʿAli to be his successor near the pond Khum. ʿAli's birthday is celebrated as are, in some Shia circles, the birthdays and the death anniversaries of all twelve *imāms*. Most importantly, and remembered everywhere, is Husain's death in Kerbela on 10 Muharram. Numerous saints' anniversaries, which depend upon local customs, can be added to this list.

The Law

A short while after the expansion of the empire began, Muslims realized that even the Koran and tradition together could not solve all controversial problems, in particular juridical and ritual ones. For with Islamic rule constantly expanding into areas where customs and traditions were completely different both from those in ancient Arabia and those envisaged in the revelation, conflicts could easily arise between the old and the new order. One observes similar difficulties even today with so many Muslims in the western world, where the problem of adjusting Islamic law (especially family status law) to modern juridical theories and practice plays an important role.

Early Muslims understood well that further development was needed. Either one tried to found new ways based solely on the two existing sources, the Koran and *ḥadīth*, or one was forced to introduce the method of analogy, *qiyās*; or one had to turn to speculation based on human reasoning, *raʾy*. In the two centuries after the Prophet's death, four legal schools, *madhhabs*, "way," appeared in which different methods were developed for the solution of emerging problems in the community.

The oldest school is that of the Iraqi Abu Hanifa (d. 767), who left more room to speculation than the others. His *madhhab*, the Hanafites, spread mainly among Turkish peoples and in large parts of Muslim India. Slightly later appears Malik ibn Anas (d. 795) in Medina, as a representative of the more traditionalist tendencies in the Prophet's city, which considered itself the guardian of his *Sunna*. Malik composed a first book on legal problems, the *Muwaṭṭaʾ*, and his school spread mainly in the western part of the Islamic empire. A disciple of both Abu Hanifa and Malik was Shafiʿi (d. 820), who took the first step toward a systematization of Islamic law, and whose school is important not only in the central Islamic areas, Egypt and Syria, but also in Africa, southern India, and Indonesia. The fourth scholar with whom a *madhhab* is connected, Ahmad ibn Hanbal (d. 855) is a pure traditionalist rather than a speculative jurist, and his unceasing struggle against the Muʿtazila in the question of whether or not the Koran was God's uncreated word secured him a place of pride among mainstream Muslims. His followers felt strictly bound to the word of the Koran and the Prophetic tradition. Their greatest representative in the later Middle Ages, Ibn Taimiyya (d. 1328), is one of the most influential figures in the annals of rigid literalism. The Hanbalites, although active in Iran and Iraq, concentrated in Central Arabia, where Muhammad ibn ʿAbdal-Wahhab revived them in the eighteenth century. From that time, the Wahhabis, supported by the clan Saʿud in Inner Arabia, have presented Hanbalism in its most unbending form and reject all 'innovations' such as the veneration of saints and mysticism (although two of the major Muslim mystics belonged to the *madhhab*) Smoking and similar innovations are prohibited.

The four schools have always existed side by side. In earlier centuries several other *madhhab* were active, which were slowly integrated into the main schools. Among them were the Zahirites, who emphasized the external, *ẓāhir*, meaning of the Koranic word. Their founder, Muhammad

ibn Da'ud (d. 909) was a fine literateur, and in the following two centuries the school boasted the most fascinating
theoretician of "chaste love," Ibn Hazm of Cordova (d.
1064), and probably influenced Ibn 'Arabi, the great master
of theosophical Sufism (d. 1240).

The Muslims never tried to unite the *madhhab*s or to
unify their teaching, for a *ḥadīth* states: "Difference of
opinion in my community is a sign of Divine mercy." Besides, the differences between the schools are generally
minimal. For example, if a person touches the skin of someone of the opposite sex, as in shaking hands, he or she has
to perform the lesser ablution, *wuḍū'*, according to three
of the schools, while Abu Hanifa does not consider that
necessary.

The theological schools, madrasah, which were
founded and developed in the eleventh century, often contained room for members and judges of all four legal
schools. Did not the Prophet say: "My community will
never agree on an error"? This saying points to the importance of *ijmā'*, the consensus of the community, for besides
the Koran, tradition, and analogy, *ijmā'* became the fourth
source of legislation. It guarantees the authenticity of the
Koran and tradition. Theoretically, *ijmā'* cannot abrogate
any text of the tradition, but, according to the view of later
jurists, it can show that the custom mentioned in earlier
sources is no longer practiced. Not the caliph but the community as a whole inherits the Prophet's wisdom, according to Sunnite doctrine. As Santillana writes:

> When the Muslim community agrees to a religious practice
> or rule of faith, it is, in a certain manner, directed and in-
> spired by God, preserved from error, and infallibly led to-
> wards the Truth . . . by virtue of a special grace bestowed
> by God upon the community of Believers.

Thus, the scholars of the Law, the *'ulamā'* (pl. of *'ālim*,
"who knows") become the preservers of tradition, and have
in this capacity even been regarded as a kind of clergy.

In the beginning *ijmā'* was a vehicle of creativity, al-
lowing new developments and the incorporation of customs

from other traditions or from local usage. However, as early as the late tenth and early eleventh centuries, it seems to have congealed and became reified, and, instead of encouraging adaptation to changing conditions, rather slowed change. Scholars were no longer supposed to investigate the Koran and *ḥadīth* independent of tradition in order to find new solutions for new problems; rather, many people claimed that "the door of *ijtihād* (individual investigation into the sources) was closed," and whatever had been accepted through *ijmāʿ* had to remain valid once for all as it was formulated. As a result of this development, many medieval practices, customs, and ideas were preserved and carried through the ages to hamper adaptation in many areas. For this reason, Ibn Taimiyya in the Middle Ages and, some five centuries after him, Modernists in India, Egypt, and Turkey tried to tear down the walls of *ijmāʿ* by going back to the Koran and the *sunna* of the earliest time, interpreting these sources afresh in the light of their, and our, time. Thus they aimed at freeing Islam from its increasing fossilization under the crust of decisions and interpretations formulated centuries earlier.

All activity of the Muslim is built into the texture of the *sharīʿa*, which discusses the believer's duties toward God and his fellow beings. The *sharīʿa*, the "broad path, the highway," can be described as "the entirety of Divine commands concerning human actions," for God is the sole legislator. It has even been claimed—doubtlessly exaggerating—that the Koran revealed only God's law but not God Himself.

The science that deals with the *sharīʿa*, is called *fiqh*, "insight," that is, understanding law based on theology. As Islam looks to everything in life from the viewpoint of religion, the *sharīʿa*, logically, comprises the religious and cultic duties as well as rules for private and common law. One distinguishes in this respect between *farḍ al-ʿain*, the duty which each and every single person, man and woman, is required to perform, e.g., ritual prayer, or fasting; and *farḍ al-kifāya*, a duty that is fulfilled by the participation of a sufficient number of believers, such as the Friday prayer in the mosque or *jihād*, the so-called "holy war." Further-more, it indicates who is "burdened," *mukallaf*, with the execution of this or that duty, for example, the healthy, ma-jor male, or a child after reaching the age of discretion. Muslims soon felt that it was well nigh impossible to fulfill all the requirements of the *sharīʿa*. Nevertheless, one has to acknowledge the binding force of the legally pre-scribed duties, and even if a Muslim does not perform a certain duty or heed certain prohibitions but knows and ad-mits that he is doing something against the *sharīʿa*, he is still considered a Muslim. But to deny the validity of the *sharīʿa* is not permitted. One can fully agree with H.A.R. Gibb's remark:

> No great religious community has ever possessed more fully the catholic spirit or been more ready to allow the widest freedom to its members provided only that they accepted, at least outwardly, the minimum obligations of the faith.

Religious practice in Islam is more important than clinging to dogmatic formulas—excepting of course the belief in the One and Unique God and the position of Muhammad as God's final messenger. This has led some orientalists to prefer the term "orthopraxis" to "orthodoxy" when speaking of Islam.

The *sharīʿa* was never codified. Forming "the prac-tical aspect of Muhammad's religious teaching" and hence indispensable for the community, it has been transmitted through the centuries from generation to generation. The religious judge, the *qāḍī*, had to supervise its execution; the *muftī* had to give a "legal opinion," *fatwā*, as to whether a certain action was lawful or unlawful. (Collections of *fatwās*, as they exist in different countries, allow interesting insights into the problems with which Muslims were faced at different times.) The office of *muftī* or Grand Muftī gained special importance in the Ottoman Empire.

In cities and areas where several *madhhab*s were rep-resented, *qāḍī*s of each school would judge independently.

But it might well happen that someone accepted the opinion of a *madhhab* other than his own, provided that his or her special case was served better by resorting to another school.

It is not surprising that the customary law, *ʿurf, ʿādat*, of the different peoples in distant areas of the Muslim world never ceased, and many problems not mentioned in the *sharīʿa*, could be solved by resorting to such local law. The juridical part of the *sharīʿa* was codified for the first time in the so-called *Mejelle* in the Ottoman Empire in 1869.

All actions are divided into five categories: obligatory, desirable or recommended, indifferent, objectionable, and prohibited. For instance, ablution before prayer is obligatory; to begin with the right side of the body is recommended; whether to use warm or cold water is indifferent, but it is prohibited that someone should have touched the water before one uses it. Besides this religious evaluation, actions are classified as to whether they are valid or invalid.

In the juridical parts of the *sharīʿa* a highly complex law of inheritance attracts the scholar's attention. In contrast to ancient Arabian practices, according to which only agnates were entitled to inherit, Islam gave women certain rights, although the testator's daughters receive a smaller fraction of the inheritance than the sons, because they were entitled to receive a dowry at the time of marriage besides their inherited share, and do not have to look after a family as the man has to do.

Marital law permits the man up to four legitimate wives and as many concubines as he wants. When a slave girl (concubine) bears her master a child, she is free when he dies.

Despite these laws polygamy is not as frequent in the Islamic world as one might think. The husband has to treat equally in every respect all his wives—and that is a difficult if not impossible task. In fact, according to some modernists the very provision that all wives should be treated with absolute justice, not only in providing material comfort but also by showing the same amount of love and tenderness to all, implies the prohibition of polygamy; for, so it would seem, no one but God can act with complete justice. For middle class families the problem of equal maintenance can cause immense difficulties. However, in case of the first wife's barrenness or illness or, especially in rural areas, to facilitate the aging wife's workload, one may take a second or even third wife. Compared to the pre-Islamic position of women, Islamic legislation meant enormous progress; the woman has the right, at least according to the letter of the law, to administer the wealth she has brought into the family or earned by her own work.

In the earliest centuries of Islam, women's position was not bad at all. Only over the course of centuries was she increasingly confined to the house and forced to veil herself. Formerly, covering one's head with a veil (also generally accepted in Judaism and early Christianity) was a sign of honorable behavior and decency. That women were studiously kept away from life outside the house often resulted in their being deprived of their rights, and ideas that were basically incompatible with Koranic injunctions and statements were applied to them, e.g., as in the case of inheritance.

Veiling and rigid seclusion is largely restricted to the middle classes. Extremely conservative in this respect are women from traditional families, and (especially in Indo-Pakistan) even more *sayyid*s, the Prophet's descendants through his daughter Fatima (who have to observe a number of taboos, at least in Indo-Muslim society). In rural areas absolute seclusion and full veiling were impossible because the women had to work in the fields. The system of seclusion, nowadays generally called *purdah* (from Persian *parda*, ''veil'') is reflected in Muslim architecture: the women's quarters form a separate section or are located in the upper storeys; houses often have an inner courtyard or small backyard where women can walk or sit without being observed by non-family members. Often, a special door allows female visitors to slip into the women's quarters without being seen.

In the house, the women—especially the mother—
rule supreme, and the history of Islam shows that women
were by no means intellectually inactive: one finds female
transmitters of *ḥadīth*, leading calligraphers, and poets. As
Muhammad's first wife had supported him during the
shock caused by the first revelations, similarly his youngest
wife, ʿAʾisha, played a considerable role in the transmis-
sion of the *ḥadīth* as well as in politics. Rabiʿa of Basra (d.
801) was a highly influential mystic; and female rulers,
such as Raziya Sultana of Delhi and Shajarat ad-Durr of
Egypt in the thirteenth century, and the Begums of Bhopal
in the nineteenth and twentieth centuries, played important
roles in their countries' politics. There was also cultural influence of princesses and rulers' consorts. The female element was certainly present in Islamic culture.

When a woman marries she needs a *wālī*, "guardian,
representative." Traditionally, marriages are arranged, and
the cross-cousin marriage is frequent. This is the case especially among noble families and the *sayyids*. Although
marriages are surrounded with many popular customs and
are usually celebrated in grand style (leading to the impov-
erishment of numerous families), the most important part
of the marriage is the contract in which the sum of the
dowry and the *mahr*, the marriage gift, are stipulated; for
marriage in Islam is a simple contract, not a sacrament.
According to some legal schools the woman can include in
the contract her right to dissolve the marriage under certain
circumstances (such as misbehavior or insanity of the
husband).

In Turkey, a laicist country, the so-called *imām nikâhĭ*
is known, that is a marriage not attested by the municipality
but solely by the *imām*. It was practiced mainly in rural areas when a man wanted to take a second or third wife,
which was impossible according to the Swiss Legal Code
introduced by Ataturk in 1925. In Iran, temporary marriage, *mutʿa*, is permitted according to Shia law; its dura-
tion is fixed by contract and can last for days or years.

Generally speaking, a woman should not take a husband who is not of equal social standing, especially one

lower in rank; a *sayyid* woman should marry only a *sayyid*. While a man is allowed to marry women from among the *ahl al-kitāb*, i.e., a Christian, Jew, or Zoroastrian (in India also a Hindu), a woman must marry a Muslim. Therefore Europeans and Americans sometimes convert to Islam in order to marry a Turkish or Arab woman.

Divorce can be pronounced by the husband without his being required to explain the reason; he can take back his wife before the expiration of the legal period of waiting (three periods of menstruation). If he pronounces thrice the *ṭalāq*, the formula of divorce, the separation is final and he can remarry the same woman only after she has been married to someone else.

Slavery was not abolished by the Koran, but believers are constantly admonished to treat their slaves well. In case of illness a slave has to be looked after and well cared for. To manumit a slave is highly meritorious; the slave can ransom himself by paying some of the money he has earned while conducting his own business. Only children of slaves or non-Muslim prisoners of war can become slaves, never a freeborn Muslim; therefore slavery is theoretically doomed to disappear with the expansion of Islam. The entire history of Islam proves that slaves could occupy any office, and many former military slaves, usually recruited from among the Central Asian Turks, became military leaders and often even rulers as in eastern Iran, India (the Slave Dynasty of Delhi), and medieval Egypt (the Mamluks). Eunuchs too served in important capacities, not only as the guardians of the women's quarters, but also in high administrative and military positions.

In penal law, one distinguishes four kinds of punishments:

1. *Talio*: the culprit can be killed or mutilated if his crime (intentional murder) has been proven in a law court.
2. If the court abstains from capital punishment, the culprit has to pay the blood money, *diya*. It consists for a woman of half, for Christians and Jews of one-third, of the sum that has to be paid for a free male Muslim. In addition, an expiation is

required because the accused person has violated not only human but also Divine right.

3. Legally established punishments exist for certain crimes, such as amputation of the right hand in case of theft.

4. Finally, the judge can order punishments by legal ordinance according to human opinion. Again, one distinguishes between cases when the right of God or the right of a human being has been violated. It is recommended not to testify against someone, as far as possible, and to show mercy, if possible.

The punishment for adultery between two free adults is a hundred lashes or, according to the most rigid schools, death by stoning. However, to prove adultery four blameless witnesses are required who must have observed the act in all details—a proviso that makes it well nigh impossible to apply the full punishment. But given this proviso, it will also be very difficult to apprehend a man and declare him guilty of raping a woman as barely any witness will be found or, if the rape happens in public (gang rape) very few might be willing to testify. Of course strict rules concerning sexual relationships made it highly unlikely that a woman would ever be alone with a man who is not an immediate family member. In tribal areas it happens that a woman only suspected of any contact with a man outside the family is killed by her relatives to save the family's honor, but this custom is not based on the *shari^a*.

The part of the *shari^a* which deals with public law dwells in the first place upon definitions of state and caliphate, and has remained largely theoretical. In the beginning, the caliph, Muhammad's successor as the leader of the community in prayer and war, had barely any religious authority, which was vested in the *'ulamā'*. Sunni orthodoxy recognized that the caliph should belong to the Prophet's clan, the Quraish, but even this was not the case with the Ottoman caliph.

The caliphs lost their power in the mid-tenth century. In subsequent centuries almost the only rights the caliph possessed were to have his name mentioned in the Friday sermon and to have money minted in his name, while secular rulers in the provinces seized power, often referring to themselves as "helper of the Prince of the Believers." The Spanish Umayyads had declared themselves caliphs in 929, while in North Africa the Fatimids, who conquered Egypt in 969, founded a third caliphate, based on their claim to be the Prophet's descendants through his daughter Fatima.

When the Mongols terminated the Abbasid caliphate in Baghdad in 1258, an alleged descendant of the last Abbasid caliph fled to Cairo, where he and his descendants served to legitimate the Mamluk rule. After the Ottoman conquest of Egypt and Syria in 1516, the last "Abbasid" caliph was brought to Istanbul and, as is claimed, invested the Ottoman sultan with the caliphate. When the Crimea was ceded to Russia in the Treaty of Küçük Kaynarca in 1774, the Ottoman Sultan was styled "supreme caliph of the Muhammadans" and thus given a religious honor, i.e., the spiritual leadership of Muslims even outside the Ottoman Empire. This construction was used by Sultan Abdul Hamid I to bolster his pan-Islamic politics in the late nineteenth-century. When Mustafa Kemal (Ataturk) abolished the sultanate in Turkey after World War I, he allowed the caliphate to continue for a short while, but his reformist activities resulted in its abolition on March 3, 1924. This not only put an end to numerous speculations about the future of the caliphate but was also the death knell for the Indian Caliphate Movement, in which Indian Muslims had expressed their loyalty to the Ottoman caliph as the spiritual protector of all believers. The abortive Caliphate Movement was the first 'freedom movement' among Indian Muslims.

As for the *shariʿa*, it comprises also the Muslims' attitude toward non-Muslims. The widespread idea that Islam made its way through the world mainly through fire and sword cannot be maintained. To be sure, for a brief span of time it seemed as if *jihād*, the struggle for the faith, might become the sixth "pillar of Islam." *Jihād* means "striving [in the path of God];" the term "holy war" goes back to the Crusaders who used it for their own undertaking; it is unknown in classical Islam. But since Sura 2/257 states, "There is no compulsion in religion," *jihād* could not become a "pillar." But there is the Koranic word that Muhammad was sent raḥmatan li'l-ʿālamīn, "as a mercy for [the inhabitants of] the worlds." The early verses of the Koran had presented Muhammad as a prophet sent to his Arab compatriots who had not yet been blessed by a Divine revelation; only later did the Koran express his role in correcting those parts of the Jewish and Christian scriptures which had been altered by the followers of these religions. This idea, one can deduce, included missionary claims, e.g., to spread the true word in the world. Some of the *suras* revealed in Medina deal with the problem of warring for the sake of the true faith, but this is to be understood primarily as the fight against aggressors and apostates. But Sura 9/29 states: "Fight against those who do not believe in God nor in the Last Day, who prohibit not what God and His messenger have prohibited, and who refuse allegiance to the true faith from among those who have received the Book, until they humbly pay tribute out of hand."

Those who have received a revealed scripture are called *ahl al-kitāb*, "the people of the Book," comprising Jews, Christians, Zoroastrians, and Sabians. They should not be killed or converted by force but rather pay a certain tax. By doing so they gain the right to be protected by Muslims and are called *dhimmī*, from *dhimma*, "protection." They are therefore exempt from military service. The pagans, polytheists who have no revealed scripture, have to be fought unless they embrace Islam. The young Muhammad ibn al-Qasim, the conqueror of the Lower Indus Valley, acted therefore with great wisdom when he, in 712, declared the Hindus and Buddhists of the newly conquered provinces to be equal to the Jews and Christians in the Near East. Otherwise it would have been impossible for the small number of Muslims who were "like a pinch of salt in a big kettle" to administer the vast areas of the Indian subcontinent.

Besides the per capita tax, the *jizya*, the *dhimmīs* had to pay a certain land tax, *kharāj*. They were also expected to differ from the believers in their dress (yellow was already the color used by Jews). The *dhimmī* could not testify in a Muslim court, but non-Muslim communities had an independent administration headed by the religious leader, be it the rabbi, the bishop, or whoever might be responsible. New churches or synagogues could not be erected in Islamic lands, but there was no objection to repairing existing religious structures.

Because of the need to fight against non-Muslims, the world was divided into *dār al-islām,* "the abode of Islam," and *dār al-ḥarb,* "the abode of war." The latter term means areas that are not yet, or else no longer, under Muslim rule. In such areas Friday prayers should not be performed. This problem was frequently discussed, especially among Indian Muslims during the nineteenth century, with British rule spreading over a larger and larger area of the provinces once ruled by Muslims, and there were different opinions as to whether British India was to be regarded as *dār al-harb.* Such problems are also on the minds of some fundamentalist Muslims today in Europe and America, but the increasing number of mosques in all parts of the western world seems to prove that most Muslims today see nothing wrong with performing the Friday prayer in an environment not under Muslim rule.

Conversion by force was and still is very rare. In fact, in early times conversions were not even deemed desirable because the special taxes on the *dhimmīs* were a boon for the treasury. Conversions for practical purposes however are often mentioned, although non-Muslims were not prohibited from working in any profession. Many of them enjoyed high offices at court: Christians and Jews became highly esteemed physicians, and as financial administrators as well as secretaries they were sought after in the state bureaucracy. Christians had long experience in this field, especially in Egypt and Syria. A saying was even attributed to the Prophet that the Copts were destined to help Muslims practice true piety by rescuing them from worldly occupations. One should not forget the numerous Jewish physicians and bankers active in the Middle East—it seems typical of the situation that the Spanish Jews, when driven out of Spain in the wake of the reconquista, should have chosen the Ottoman Empire as their refuge, because the Muslim government protected them as *dhimmīs* and enabled them to continue their professions.

Most severe punishment, however, is ordered for apostasy. The *murtadd*, (''apostate'') has ''to expect God's wrath and heavy punishment.'' Thus states the Koran (Sura 16/108 et al). In numerous *ḥadīth* capital punishment is demanded for such a person; it is defined in *fiqh* as death by the sword. Apostasy under duress, as long as the heart remains firm in Islam, is not considered apostasy by most *ʿulamāʾ*. Whether or not the crime of ''slandering the Prophet'' is liable to capital punishment has been discussed for centuries.

Theology and Philosophy

The conflict between Islam and Christianity is reflected in numerous disputes and apologetic writings on both sides. The tension between the two religions was enhanced by the fact that the Koran contains several references to the life of Jesus which, of course, are accepted by the Muslims as absolute and indisputable truth as they constitute God's own word, while they contradict Christian dogma on certain points.

The Koran acknowledges the virgin birth. Jesus is the Word which God placed into Mary. This, however, does not mean that he should be called "God's Son." Rather, he is the last great prophet before Muhammad, a healer and a model of love, poverty, and humility, who never thought of claiming divine status. Mary—thus says Islamic tradition—is one of the four best women that ever lived on earth. In contrast to other children of Adam she was not touched by Satan. She is loved by the people, and the moving description of the annunciation in Maulana Rumi's great Persian epic, the *Mathnawī* (Book III, 3700 ff.) equals in tenderness the finest Christian poetry in honor of the virgin.

The Koran mentions only fragments from the life of Jesus. There, as in later traditions, scenes known from apocryphal writings are echoed, such as his capacity to grant life to clay birds by breathing upon them. This, incidentally, forms the basis for an image used thousands of times in Persian, Arabic, Turkish, and Urdu poetry: the breath or the kiss of the beloved is compared to the life-bestowing breath of Jesus. "Jesus-breathed" means simply "healing, life-giving."

But in the Koran, the crucifixion is not accepted:

> They did not kill him and did not crucify him, rather someone was made resembling him. (*Sura* 4/157).

Hence, the central importance of the Cross in Christian faith is never properly understood by a Muslim, even less so as the need for redemption is not acknowledged, because Islam does not know the concept of original sin. According to the teaching of the modern Ahmadiyya sect, Jesus wandered to Kashmir after someone else had been crucified in his place; his tomb is taken to be near Srinagar where he died at a great age. With this attitude the Ahmadiyya takes a position that is unacceptable for both Christians and Muslims.

Educated Muslims often consider modern biblical criticism to be proof of the Koranic statement that changes in both the Old and the New Testament have taken place. Prophecies about the future appearance of Muhammad are found in several passages of the Bible, especially the promise that the *paraklet* will come as a consoler some time after Christ. This remark was always regarded as a reference to Muhammad, for Sura 61/6 speaks of Ahmad "the highly praised one," in Greek *periklētos*, which Muslim scholars assume was intended by the term *paraklētos*. This highly Praised one, Ahmad or Muhammad (both come from the same root), was to bring the full and finite revelation.

The problem of the nature of Christ, so central in the dogmatic development of the early church, has also influenced, in a certain way, the development of Islamic dogma.

Christ's designation as *logos*, as the Word of God, "born not created," has most probably influenced Islamic theories about the Koran, which is regarded by the Muslim as the uncreated Word of God. Phenomenologically seen, the Koran has the same position in Islamic dogmatics as has Christ in Christianity. Harry A. Wolfson therefore coined the term "inlibration," the "Word become Book," in contrast to the Christian concept of incarnation, "the Word become Flesh." That explains why theologians emphasized the designation *ummī* for Muhammad; this term, first probably meaning "the prophet sent to the gentiles" was interpreted as "illiterate." The Prophet had to be a vessel unstained by external knowledge for the Word's inlibration, just as Mary had to be virgin in order to be a pure vessel for the Word's incarnation. That is, the Koran is much more than simply a book, and hence the Muslim can pray:

> O Lord, adorn us with the ornament of the Koran,
> and favor us through the grace of the Koran,
> and honor us through the honor of the Koran,
> and invest us with the robe of honor of the Koran
> and make us enter Paradise through the intercession of
>   the Koran
> and rescue us from all the evil in the world
>   and the pain of the Otherworld for the sake of the
>   honor of the Koran . . .
> O Lord, make the Koran for us a companion in this
>   world
> and an intimate friend in the tomb,
> and a friend at the Day of Resurrection,
> and a light on the Bridge,
> and a companion in Paradise,
> and a veil and protection from the Fire,
> and a guide to all good deeds
> by Thy grace and kindness and favor!

Yet it has to be emphasized that this high veneration of the Koran does not impair Muhammad's position; he, as the last messenger, is elevated over all other human beings, and the Muslim has a very personal relationship with him.

The problem of the Koran's nature immediately leads to some of the important issues of Islamic dogmatics. Typical of the twofold character of Islam, which embraces both *dīn wa daula*, religion and state, is a fundamental religiopolical question: that is, who is the *imām*, the leader of the community in prayer and war?

During the battle of Siffin (657), when ʿAli ibn Abi Talib, the fourth caliph, cousin and son-in-law of the Prophet, faced his adversary Muʿawiya, the future Umayyad caliph, the latter, fearing possible defeat, ordered his soldiers to place copies, or at least pages, of the Koran on their lances so that the battle might be decided through God's word. ʿAli accepted the arbitration although his victory was near, and this action led one group of Muslims to secede. For them, the question at stake was to what extent the *imām*, the leader of the community, was to be judged according to his ethical qualities; that is, the fundamental question was the relation of faith and works. The seceding party, the Kharijites (from *kharaja*, "to go out, secede") now took sides against their former leader ʿAli, as he, instead of completely relying upon God's decision, had accepted a human stratagem. The Kharijites can be called "ethical maximalists," accepting no faith without works. They therefore claim that faith can increase by good works. Cultic actions have to be performed not only in the state of external purity but also with a clear conscience. A person who commits a major sin can no longer be regarded as a Muslim and deserves eternal punishment in Hell. Among the major sins are counted idolatry, witchcraft, murder, embezzlement of the goods of orphans, usury, desertion, and rape of a Muslim woman.

These non-conformist Kharijites consisted of a rather small group of believers who mercilessly fought against those who seemed to be too lax, and they went to extremes in applying the Koranic command to "order the good and restrain people from doing evil." They felt that they were the only true believers while all the others were, due to their lukewarm attitude, infidels and had to be killed. As for the office of the caliph, it should be administered only by an absolutely impeccable Muslim "even though he may be an Abyssinian slave." Their rigor made the Kharijites split off from the mainstream, and they survived mainly in fringe areas of the Islamic world, such as parts of North Africa and Oman; these puritan groups are called Ibadi.

The people of the *Sunna* and the *jamāᶜa*, i.e., "the body of believers," that is, the Sunnites, tried to steer a middle course. H. A. R. Gibb writes:

> It would not be to go too far beyond the bounds of strict truth to say . . . that no body of religious sectarians has ever been excluded from the orthodox community but those who desired such an exclusion and as it were excluded themselves.

The principle that Gibb expresses here had its defenders even in the earliest times of Islamic history. It came to be represented mainly by the so-called Murjites, "those who postpone," whose viewpoint was diametrically opposed to that of the Kharijites (who wanted to be excluded). The Murjites held that judgment about a person's character had to be left to God. Faith, according to their viewpoint, could neither increase nor diminish by works, but is rather a matter of the heart. Furthermore, even a grave sinner is not an infidel and therefore does not deserve eternal punishment in Hell. In the Koran, problems of this kind are not treated systematically, and as Muhammad was a prophet and not a scholastic theologian, he never tried to systematize the revelations. Thus every group can find verses of the Koran or *ḥadīth* which agree with their respective opinions. This is particularly true of one question which is on the Muslims' mind to this day, i.e., predestination. Is the human being free or is each of his actions predestined? The Koran says on the one hand (Sura 3/139):

> And he who wants the reward of this world We give it to
>   him,
> and he who wants the reward of the next world, We give
>   it to him,
> and verily We recompense the grateful.

On the other hand it is stated (Sura 74/34 et al):

> Thus God leaves in error whom He will,
>   and guides right whom
> He will.

One group among the early Muslims, called Jabrites (from *jabr*, "coercion") accepted the latter Koranic statement and considered everything to be predestined, even in the minutest detail. Understandably, such an attitude pleased the Umayyad rulers because it could explain even unpopular or impious political actions simply as being predestined. (That is why many later theologians and mystics regarded predestination as an easy excuse for laziness and sins.)

On the other end of the spectrum one finds the so-called Qadarites (from *qadar*, "decree") who admitted that human beings have the capacity to act according to their own will and thus become responsible for their actions.

Between the Kharijites and the Murjites developed the Mu'tazila, "those who refrain, who separate themselves." They are those who took an intermediate attitude concerning the grave sinner; according to them, he is neither a believer nor an unbeliever.

Formerly, the Mu'tazila were often called the "free-thinkers" of Islam. This, however, was incorrect. On the contrary, their concern was deeply religious and very serious. Although they allotted a major part to reason in theological discussion, in ethics they sided with the Qadariyya; that is, they admit free will and human responsibility. One of their main problems was to protect Islam from the dualistic influences that began to seep in from Iran. During the eighth to the beginning of the tenth centuries, the Mu'tazila with their numerous branches took an extremely important step toward the development of Islamic dogma. The challenge before them was to find a compromise between the simple pious tradition, as it was centered in Medina from the days of the Prophet, and the exigencies of a refined civilization influenced by hellenistic traditions. With the expansion of the Islamic empire Muslims were exposed to many cultural, literary, political, and religious traditions in the newly conquered areas, and this posed a good number of problems for scholars. Thus, the formulation of the simple, clear statements of the Koran and *ḥadīth* into philosophically acceptable dogmatic forms was required.

The first great theological threat in the Islamic areas, especially in Iraq, now the seat of the caliphate, was Iranian dualism. Manichean infiltration apparently played a certain role in the emergence of these trends, as Manicheism has been in the air for several centuries in the Middle East. During the years 784–785 a persecution of heretics called *zindīq* (from *zand*, the commentary of the sacred Zoroastrian scripture, the Avesta) took place. To counteract the Iranian dualist tendencies, the Muʿtazila emphasized the need to formulate the profession of God's unity, *tauḥīd*, in the most decisive form possible. For them, *tauḥīd* meant that any similarity between God and his creation is absolutely impossible (contrary to the naive anthropomorphism of the traditionalist school, where Koranic terms such as "God's Face" or "God descends" seem to have been understood literally). Such Koranic anthropomorphism, the Muʿtazilites insisted, has to be interpreted allegorically. As for the Divine Attributes, they are identical with the Divine Essence. Nothing that is co-eternal could exist with God, for that would an impairment of His Unity and Unicity. Hence it has to be postulated that His hearing, seeing, speaking, etc., cannot be primordial, for then something besides Him would have existed from pre-eternity. Logically, then, the Koran cannot be the uncreated Word of God but must be a created quiddity. It was this very point which led to the long, fierce theological battle between the Muʿtazila and those who upheld the traditional, old-fashioned creedal position.

The second important aspect of the Muʿtazilite doctrine is Divine Justice, *ʿadl*. God *must* act justly; He cannot repay humans with evil for good; even animals have to be recompensed in the Other World for injustice done to them here on earth. However, justice is measured according to human reason; thus one is faced with the danger that man is free while God, fettered by His own Justice, is not free. In 827 the Abbasid caliph Ma'mun accepted the Mu'tazilite doctrine officially, and it remained in power under the following two caliphs. Those who upheld the traditional position, especially Ahmad ibn Hanbal, were persecuted; even more, those who did not understand the sophisticated Mu'tazilite dogmatic definitions or refused to accept them were sometimes treated almost as infidels. The Mu'tazilites replaced the warmth of personal religious faith with intellectual speculation. Then in the reign of Mutawakkil, the power of the Mu'tazilites was broken and their doctrine that the Koran was created was regarded as heresy.

The vehement spiritual struggle between the two currents was overcome to a certain extent by al-Ash'ari (d. 935), who had his roots in the Mu'tazila and thus was able to fight his old school with its own weapons; that is, he introduced sophisticated scholastic reasoning into traditionalist circles. In the eastern part of the Islamic world Maturidi worked on similar lines. The belief in the Uncreated Koran had won the day: whatever is inside the binding (''between the two covers'') of the book is God's uncreated word, though our pronunciation of the words is created.

Al-Ash'ari's doctrine can be called a typical mediating theology. It teaches that God cannot be imagined according to human categories of thought; that His hand, His face, and His movements as mentioned in the Koran are to be understood *bilā kaifa*, ''without How''; that human beings are neither completely free nor completely unfree but ''acquire'' the acts predestined for them and thus appropriate them and are judged accordingly. Events appear to us to be following normal laws of cause and effect, but in reality it is only the Divine custom, *sunna*, *'āda*, which brings forth from time immemorial the same results from the same causes. If this sequence is interrupted, a miracle takes place which is called, typically, *khāriq ul-'āda*, ''what tears apart the custom.'' A good example of this attitude, often told in early Arabic and Persian sources, is the story of a Persian

Sufi who wanted to prove to a fire worshiper that fire can burn only with God's permission. In trance he passed through a burning pyre without injuries, except for a small burn on his foot which happened as he came out of his trance at the last step. For a modern mind this constitutes a perfect example of the power of ecstasy, but for the pious spectators in the tenth century it could be offered as proof that God can break His custom whenever He pleases.

The development of the Ash'arite viewpoint clearly reflects the religious or political dangers that had to be avoided or countered. One also observes a progressive hardening of the formulas of the creed as well as an increasingly refined scholastic conceptualization of theological terms. The *mutakallim*, the speculative theologian, became an important and respected member of the religious establishment. The scholastic way of thinking and arguing developed in the Middle Ages is still applied by many traditionally educated Muslims when they want to prove the rationality of their religion, and the modern Western scholar, usually no longer acquainted with this way of thinking, often has difficulties when discussing theological themes with a Muslim. (That a bus driver in Turkey once asked me whether the profession of faith should not be called the "foundation of religion" rather than the first "pillar of Islam" shows that this kind of approach can permeate the attitude of even a "simple" Muslim.)

The profession of faith means to acknowledge God's Unity and Muhammad's role as the final prophet, who is charged with the application of the God-given order. There exists, however, an enlarged form which is generally learned by rote and often written in calligraphic "pictures" (such as the "boat of salvation" in Turkey). The generally accepted form was formulated in the *Fiqh Akbar*. It says:

> I believe in God and His angels, His books, and His messengers and the resurrection after death and the predestination by God, good as well as evil, and the Judgment, the Scales, Paradise and Hellfire—all this is truth.

The belief in the prophets comprises all divinely sent messengers from Adam and Abraham, Moses and Jesus, to Muhammad, for God has never left the world without guidance. The number of these messengers, some of whom are singled out as lawgivers, is usually given as twenty-eight. Yet it is possible to also accept messengers not mentioned in the Koran, provided they have lived and taught before the time of Muhammad. That means, theoretically, a Muslim can regard the Buddha or Confucius as prophets. The revealed books, according to the Koran, include the Torah, the Psalms, the Gospel, and the Koran.

The belief in angels plays an important role in theology but even more in popular faith. It is supported by numerous statements in the Koran. Gabriel occupies the most important position among the angels; he is styled the Holy Spirit or the Trustworthy Spirit. It was he who conveyed the Divine message to the Prophet. Michael, according to popular belief, controls the forces of nature and the allotment of nourishment. These two angels are extremely tall, and so is Israfil, whose head reaches the Divine Throne while his feet are posited beneath the seventh earth. He has four wings. When just before Doomsday all creatures, including angels, will die, Israfil will be the first to be resurrected so that he can sound the trumpet to summon everyone for the Judgment. More terrible and awesome than all angels and spiritual powers, however, is 'Azra'il, the angel of death. Of cosmic dimensions, he has 4,000 wings, all beset with tongues and eyes. As soon as someone's death is written on the tablet of Divine decrees, he grasps that person's soul to tear it out, cruelly if he deals with an infidel, but carefully when he takes that of a believer. In the grave the dead person has to face two examiner angels, Munkar and Nakir, who interrogate him and, if necessary, punish him. For this reason one likes to whisper the profession of faith into a dying person's ear so that he or she can answer correctly the angel's questions.

Humans are surrounded and protected by angels during their whole lifetime, and the pious believe in the presence of two, sometimes four, or sometimes even a whole hosts of protecting angels. Two recording angels are placed on one's shoulders: the angel on the right shoulder notes down the believer's good actions, while the one on the left takes notes of his evil actions. However, the angel on the left hesitates a while before completing his work, and if the sinner repents during a certain span of time, his mistakes and sins are not entered in the record.

The numerous angels who are busy supervising the course of the world and the life of human beings can act only according to God's order. Besides them, the heavenly hosts, whose number cannot be counted, devote themselves exclusively to the praise of God. Sometimes they are described as organized in classes according to the seven spheres; at the summit four heavenly beings carry the Throne of God. The angels are restricted in their activities; each of them knows only one single formula of laud and praise, which he repeats from eternity to eternity, and only one position of prayer. Nineteen angels serve as overseers of Hell.

Muhammad refused to say anything about the gender of the angels and turned in particular against the belief of the Meccans that angels or angelic beings are God's daughters. Angels, according to the general opinion, are created from light and consist of a simple, uncompounded, hence incorruptible, subtle substance. They know only what God allows them to know, and lack the possibility for development.

Besides believing in angels, the Muslim also believes in the existence of jinns, spiritual beings of undefined character, able to acknowledge and accept positive values and sometimes even capable of embracing Islam. Their existence is officially acknowledged in the Koran (Sura 72), so much so that even the possibility of marriage between humans and jinns is discussed among scholars. In ancient Arabia they were known as spirits present in the natural world and were thought to inspire soothsayers and poets, but also to cause madness: *majnūn*, "mad" means obsessed by a jinn. These creatures have subclans, e.g., the female desert

spirit, *ghūl*, that often shows itself in animal shape, for instance as a wild cat.

Iblis, *diabolos*, the devil, is usually regarded as a
fallen angel or as a jinn, since the Koran says that he, like
the jinn, was made from fire. As he refused to prostrate
himself before the newly created Adam, he was exiled from
Paradise. Generally, his refusal to bow down before a creature is explained by his pride: since he was created from
fire, he claimed to be superior to Adam, who was created
from clay. Besides, he had served and worshiped God from
pre-eternity, surpassing all angels in works of obedience.
Some mystics interpret his refusal to bow down as an expression of overstressed *tauḥīd*: he found it impossible and
illicit to venerate anything besides God and failed to recognize the Divine breath which God had breathed into
Adam to grant him superiority over every other creature. In
the mystical current inaugurated by Hallaj Iblis is "more
monotheist than God Himself," as Hellmut Ritter phrased
it. He assumes the role of the suffering lover who prefers to
accept God's curse rather than disobey His eternal command, which prohibits obeisance to anyone but Him. In any
case, Iblis remains the enemy of human beings, always re-
taining, however, a certain relationship with God, who has
created him too. He never becomes completely anti-divine.
That means one deals not with the Iranian dualism of absolute Good and absolute Evil, but rather with the old
Semitic concept of Satan as an instrument of God.

At Doomsday, the actions of all human beings are
weighed by God's power on enormous scales whose
weights are mustard seeds. The Book of a person's actions
is given into his hand—the right one, if he is without sin,
the left one if he is a sinner; or else the Book itself is
weighed. Across Hell's back leads a bridge, *ṣirāṭ*, which is
thinner than a hair and sharper than a sword; the infidels'
feet slide so that they fall into Hell, while the believers will
walk without difficulty to reach the eternal abode safely. At
Doomsday God treats people differently; some are subject
to a rigid reckoning; some are treated with mercy and kindness; others again (in the first place martyrs) enter Paradise

without any reckoning. God asks whomsoever He chooses among the prophets whether and how they have promulgated His message, and whomsoever He chooses from among the infidels why they have refused to believe in His message. Those who have introduced innovations He will interrogate about the *sunna*, and Muslims in general about their works. Those believing in God's unity will be brought out of the fire after being punished for their sins, so that finally no one who believes in God's unity will remain in Hell. Intercessors for sinners and transgressors among Muslims will be the prophets, then the religious scholars, then the martyrs, then the other believers; those for whom no intercessor pleads will be saved from Hell solely by God's grace. Anyone whose heart contains just a single grain of faith will be saved from Hell.

The concepts concerning the punishments in the next world developed over a long time. Their basis is given in many Koranic passages, such as Sura 11/108–109:

> The damned ones enter the fire . . . to remain therein as long as heaven and earth exist, except if God should decree otherwise.

The conviction that those slain for the sake of faith (*shahīd*, "martyr") will enter Paradise without interrogation and will expect resurrection in a special place of Paradise is based on Sura 3/163: "Do not think that those slain for the sake of their Lord are dead, rather they are alive with their Lord."

Theological views concerning eternal punishment differ. In most early views they were considered to be literally true. The Muʿtazilites regarded them as a logical corollary of God's justice. For this reason al-Ashʿari accused them of depriving people of hope in God's mercy. Abu Hanifa considered heaven and Hell as realities never to disappear; later, al-Qastallani refuted this view with the Koranic dictum that "Everything is passing but the Face of God" (Sura 28/88, cf. 55/26).

Slowly, the milder interpretation gained the upper hand, all the more as hope for the Prophet's intercession for his community became more and more important in Muslim piety. Many pious souls found consolation in an alleged Prophetic saying which states that "there will be a day when the gates of Hell are muddy and watercress grows from its soil." For their part, philosophers and mystics have spiritualized the images of Paradise and Hell as glowing or terrifying images appropriate for simple believers; they interpreted them as states of the soul, or as symbols of a truth that cannot be expressed without concrete pictures. True eternal happiness is the *visio beatifica*, the vision of God and the experience of the soul's never-ending penetration into the infinite depth of the Divine, or how one might describe the ineffable mystery of Eternal Life.

Discussions between the various theological currents, as well as increasing contacts with foreign religions as the Muslim empire expanded, inspired, in the tenth and eleventh centuries, a number of Arabic works that deal with the peculiarities of the different sects and religions within and beyond the Islamic world. Among them is a basic work by al-Ashʿari, a critical study of the Spaniard Ibn Hazm (d. 1064), and one by the Persian scholar Shahrastani (d. 1153). The Khwarezmian al-Biruni (d. 1048), who lived in Ghazna (now Afghanistan) at the time when Sultan Mahmud conquered large parts of Northwest India, devoted himself to the study of Indian religions and philosophy. His *Kitāb al-Hind* ("on India") is based on a solid study of both language and philosophy; it can well be regarded as the first objective book ever written on the history of religion. Biruni is one of the most important representatives of Islamic scholarship; his work on the calendars of different nations is still indispensable; in his work Muslim scientific studies culminate, having made enormous progress from the early ninth century.

One of the intellectual areas with which early Muslim scholars had to cope was philosophy. In the first phase they attempted to combine logically, or at least reconcile, Greek philosophical thought and Islamic dogma. The Muʿtazila made the first steps in this field, and it is possible to establish a certain connection between this theological movement and the so-called "philosopher of the Arabs," al-Kindi (d. 870). He was a representative of the exact sciences; for the first time he emphasized the world of reason, where alone freedom and immortality were to be found. Furthermore, he accepted the Neo-platonic doctrine of the emanation of individual souls from the Universal Soul, which in turn emerges from the Divine Principle.

One characteristic trait of early Islamic philosophy is the belief that there is fundamentally no difference between Plato and Aristotle; this viewpoint is clearly expressed in the writings of Aristotle's first great commentator, the Central Asian al-Farabi (d. 950 in Aleppo). He, as well as his successors, claimed the unity of philosophy and Islamic revelation, and taught that God creates the world by His thinking.

Ibn Sina, physician and philosopher (famed in the West as Avicenna) (d. 1037), continued the ideas of his predecessors: God is the *prima causa*, and everything that might possibly exist has its essential pre-existence in God's knowledge. The great thinker al-Ghazzali, representing the Ash'arite stance, harshly criticized this doctrine, which postulated the eternity of the world as it existed essentially from the very beginning in God's knowledge; he also attacked the philosopher's negation of individual immortality. Therefore Ibn Sina was regarded among certain mystics in the Muslim East as a rationalist who denied Muhammad's role as the mediator between mankind and God, although his own work contains some mystical trends as well.

The idea that philosophical knowledge and Divine revelation fully agree is poetically expressed in the philosophical novel *Hayy ibn Yaqzān* by Ibn Tufail (d. 1184), vizier and court physician at the court of the North African Almohads. This novel describes the development of a child who, exposed on a lonely island, slowly develops in periods of seven years through all stages of human life, rising to ever higher spiritual insight until he reaches the summit of pure contemplation. Then, when he compares the results of his spiritual experience with those preached by the prophets in a nearby country, he realizes that both agree with each other perfectly.

Ibn Tufail's successor at the court of the Almohads was Ibn Rushd, known in the West as Averroes (d. 1198). He further elaborated the doctrine of the fundamental agreement between philosophy and revelation. Philosophy has to explain the truth of the prophets' messages in a more sophisticated form, and humankind has to be instructed in one way or another according to their capacity of understanding. This doctrine, which became both famous and infamous (due to an inaccurate translation) as "double truth" was attacked by both Muslim and Christian theologians, some Christians using al-Ghazzali's refutation of the philosophers as one of their weapons. Contrary to the views of earlier philosophers, Averroes teaches that matter has no beginning; creation does not consist of a singular passage from potentiality to actuality but happens every moment. The goal of human beings is the unification of the material intellect with the active First Intellect, as can be seen in great human beings of history; thus immortality is secured for leading spirits.

Among later Muslim philosophical thinkers, Ibn Khaldun (d. 1406) deserves pride of place; he has been styled the "first sociologist," not only in Islam but in all of history. His fundamental concept is that of *ʿaṣabiyya*, the *esprit de corps*, common activity, or group spirit. The *ʿaṣabiyya* is a tremendously important socio-psychological factor which, combined with religious zeal, can lead a people to victory over others. Ibn Khaldun shows how states grow, reach their zenith after some three generations, and then spread out too far, weakening and waning, while at their borders new, young states emerge, which wax and wane in the same rhythm. This process repeated itself time and again in Islamic history.

In medieval Islamic society natural sciences and medicine occupied an important place. The scientific achievements of medieval Muslims are especially remarkable: they not only translated, reworked, and enlarged the Greek sources at their disposal, but by doing so they essentially formed the bases for modern exact science. Avicenna's work on medicine was used in Europe for many centuries. Numerous concepts in science reveal an Arabo-Islamic heritage—the names of stars, and mathematical terms like "algebra" and "algorithm," as well as Arabic numerals which, like zero, originated in India and were brought to the West by the Muslims. Without these mathematical tools, modern mathematics could not have developed. Optics and geometry are also part of the Islamic heritage, and the infinite varieties of artistic geometrical design in decoration and in the construction of stalactites show Muslim skill in highly complicated mathematical problems. These very sciences, transferred by the Arabs into Western Europe, enabled European scientists, with the help of modern technology, to reach an enormous advantage over the Middle Eastern countries. One therefore understands when Muslim modernists voice the idea that Western science and technology should not be imitated externally but, as Muslims did in the Middle Ages during their encounter with Greek science, should be adopted and interpreted as part and parcel of the Muslims' own heritage which they had failed, in post-medieval times, to appropriate and develop.

The Shia and
Related Sects

The battle of Siffin in 657 is not only the starting point for
the development of Islamic dogmatics but also for the emergence of different sects—or rather, for the cleavage of the
Muslim community into two major branches.

'Ali's close partisans constituted the *shī'at 'Ali,*
"'Ali's party.'' Along with the general Islamic belief in Allah, Muhammad and his message, and the uncreated Koran, the Shiites believe in the *imām* as the true leader of the
faithful and the veritable interpreter of the Koran. According to Shia doctrine, Muhammad, shortly before his death,
appointed 'Ali as the leader of the community and initiated
him into the esoteric aspects and the mysteries of faith, and
certain designated descendants in turn inherited this func-
tion. However, the belief in the specific rank and office of
'Ali's family is expressed in different forms. Thus, one can
simply acknowledge one of his descendants, either through
Hasan or Husain, as the true *imām* (that was the attitude of

91

the Zaidites), but one may also believe in the embodiment of a luminous divine substance in the *imām*, nay even in the divine incarnation of ʿAli and his descendants. It is said that ʿAli himself was almost religiously venerated by some of his partisans, an attitude he greatly disliked and disapproved of. By tradition (not only in the Shiite version but in the general Islamic one as well), he appears as the supreme hero who vanquishes enemies of the faith with his miracle-working double-edged sword Dhuʾl-fiqar and guides believers to a deeper understanding of the Koranic revelation. He is the Prophet's intimate and trusted friend and his true heir; for his sake the sun stopped so that he could perform his prayer, and more than a thousand miracles are attributed to him. Numerous adages and wise sayings bear his name, for the Prophet claimed "I am the city of wisdom and ʿAli is its gate." Even more, he is the "saint," the "friend of God", *walī Allāh,* par excellence, and the Shia have in relatively recent times added these words to the generally pronounced two-part formula of the *shahāda.*

The death of Husain, the younger son of ʿAli and Fatima, in the battle of Kerbela on 10 Muharram 680 enriched the Shia world view with the passion motif, and through the ages poetry and prose have resounded with laments about the tragic fate of the Prophet's beloved grandson. To weep for him was considered highly meritorious—rather, it was the key to Paradise. Fatima assumed the role of the *mater dolorosa.* (From a strictly chronological view she had passed away nearly fifty years before her son's death.) The sense of tragedy among the Shiites never abated, all the more as other members of the ʿAlid family too were later persecuted or killed.

Strangely, however, the first germs of the ideas that were to become typical of Shiite theology centered not around ʿAli or one of his two sons from Fatima (that is, the real grandsons of the Prophet) but rather around ʿAli's son from another woman, Muhammad ibn al-Hanafiyya, who died in 684. A partisan of Muhammad, Mukhtar, spread the news that he had not died but was alive somewhere in the mountains and would return as the *mahdi* before the Day of

Judgment "to fill the earth with justice as it is now filled with injustice." Soon, the belief in the return of Muhammad ibn al-Hanafiyya was transferred to other members of the ʿAlid house; more correctly, to that member who was considered by his followers to be the final *imām*, be it the fifth, the seventh, or the twelfth.

In the beginning the interest of the *shiʿat ʿAli* concentrated upon Husain's descendants. His son Zain al-ʿAbidin was one of the few survivors of the battle of Kerbela. Among his male children, Zaid was killed in 740. The so-called Zaidiyya, who are close to Sunnis in theology and practice, regard him as the last *imām*, the fifth in the sequence beginning with ʿAli. They do not care whether the leader of the community is a descendant of Hasan or of Husain. Formerly active near the Caspian Sea, the Zaidis ruled in Yemen for centuries and were overthrown only recently.

The other Shia groups recognized as fifth *imām* not Zaid but his brother Muhammad al-Baqir, whose son Jaʿfar as-Sadiq (d. 765) is regarded as the founder of that legal school which was accepted by the Twelver Shia (*ithnā ʿasharī shīʿa*); he also played a role in the development of mystical ideas. After Jaʿfar's death, however, a new schism occurred. Twelver Shia, which is today Iran's official religion, continued the line through Musa al-Kazim to the twelfth *imām,* Muhammad al-Mahdi who, it is said, absconded as a small child in 874. The so-called Sevener Shia took Musa's brother Ismaʿil to be the next *imām* and is therefore called, at least in their most important strand, the Ismailiyya.

Twelver Shia has been the state religion in Iran since 1501. It is based upon the belief in the hidden *imām* who rules over time from the Unseen; his theological position is interpreted in his absence by the *mujtahids,* religious scholars. Understandably, there is no acceptance of *ijmāʿ* as in the Sunni tradition. Contrary to frequent claims, Shiites do not deny the validity of the *sunna,* the tradition and customs of the Prophet. Rather, they acknowledge it even more rigidly in some ways than the Sunnites, although they emphasize, naturally, traditions of pro-Alid character. In dogmatics, the Twelver Shia or Imamiyya is rather close to some of the Mu'tazilite viewpoints. In certain aspects they are stricter than the Sunnites (for example, the infidel is regarded as ritually impure). According to Shia doctrine the *imām* is the depository of a luminous, divine substance, inherited from generation to generation. However, the question remains open whether the father invests as his successor the son in whom the light becomes manifest or whether it is inherited automatically by the first-born son.

The tombs of the *imāms* and their family members, especially Kerbela, Najaf, Qum, Kazimain, and Mashhad, are frequent pilgrimage sites; pious Shiites hope to be buried there in order to participate in the *imām*'s spiritual radiance. Small tablets and prayer beads made from the clay of Kerbela in particular are thought to convey blessings. The influence of the Shia increased in the course of time in India; many rulers in the Deccan (Golconda) and in Awadh (Lucknow) belonged to the Twelver Shia, and literature as well as customs in these places reflect a typical Shiite attitude. After partition, a considerable number—perhaps 15 percent—of the Muslims in Pakistan are Shiites. Turkey and northern Syria have Shia sectarian minorities.

The most fascinating group is the so-called Sevener Shia, which traces itself back to Ja'far's son Isma'il (d. ca. 765). Members of "Ismaili" groups, within which one must differentiate among various currents, irritated the Islamic world considerably during the Middle Ages. The Qarmathians, called after their initiator Hamdan Qarmat, consider Isma'il's son Muhammad the last *imām*. Qarmathian propaganda began in the ninth century from Kufa, 'Ali's old stronghold; then their center was shifted to al-Ahsa in the Arabian desert. The Qarmathians were accused by their adversaries of a kind of religious communism, as often happens with unorthodox sects. In 930 they succeeded in carrying off the black stone of the Ka'ba; no pilgrimage could be performed for twenty-two years until the stone was brought back. At the same time, Qarmathians founded a small state around Multan in the southern Punjab.

The Qarmathians believed in the possibility of an ascending perception of Divine truths by initiation and gradual development. They blended basic Islamic concepts with Neo-platonic and gnostic ideas, teaching the evolution of the human being, who is regarded as a microcosm which descends from the Universal Intellect through the World Soul to human intelligence and the 'tenebrous light.' Life after death, when mankind is finally rescued from the influences of nature and the ever-revolving spheres, will be a result of man's conduct on earth: the good will live in a sphere of purity while the evil will roam about without rest beneath the lunar sphere.

Needless to say, people with such an understanding of religion did not interpret the Koran in its literal sense. Therefore it is not wrong to call the Qarmathians, along with other Sevener Shiites, *bāṭiniyya,* "the people of the inner meaning," *bāṭin,* because step by step disciples are led along complicated ways into the esoteric truth of the sacred Book. One of the greatest representatives of Ismaili philosophy, the Persian author Nasir-i Khusrau (d. sometime after 1072 in Yumghan, northern Afghanistan) has beautifully characterized this interiorization of the duties of a Muslim:

> The external meaning of prayer, *ṣalāt,* is to worship God through one's corporeal attitude by turning one's body toward the prayer direction of the bodies, which is the Ka'ba, the sanctuary of the Most High, which is situated in Mecca. The spiritual meaning of prayer, however, is to worship God through one's thinking soul by turning toward the prayer direction of the spirits in order to receive the pure knowledge of the sacred Book and the Divine Law. The prayer direction of the spirits is the House of God, the abode in which the Divine knowledge dwells, and that is the *imām* of the truth, peace be upon him.

This means that the living *imām* is the true center of religion.

Ismaili currents inspired the movement of the Fatimids who, after a brief stay in North Africa at the very beginning of the tenth century, slowly began to move eastward. They conquered Egypt in 969 to create an empire that lasted for two centuries. The most famed among the Fatimid rulers is al-Hakim (who apparently suffered from mental instability). He disappeared mysteriously in 1021, four years after his partisans had declared that he was a Divine incarnation. The major propagandist of this idea was one Isma'il ad-Darazi, along with a Persian author, Hamza. The Druzes, living to this day in Jabal Hauran and Lebanon, are called after ad-Darazi. They believe in the return of the Divine caliph al-Hakim but have adapted themselves almost completely to the ruling form of religion as practiced around them. (*Taqiyya,* ''hiding one's faith in times of danger,'' is part of Shia ethics.)

After the death of the caliph Mustansir in 1094, the Fatimid line split. The Egyptians followed Mustansir's younger son Musta'li, while the real heir apparent, Nizar, was forced to flee. He and his young son were invited by Hasan-i Sabbah to the mountain fortress of Alamut in Iran and protected there. From this fortress the so-called Assassins came: these were faithful disciples of Hasan, who, blindly devoted to their master, performed political assassinations, usually by sacrificing themselves too. The word ''assassin'' is probably a distortion of *ḥashshā-shiyyūn,* ''eater of hashish.'' However, as only inimical reports about their activities and alleged brutalities are known, much of the early history of the Alamut period is still shrouded in mystery. In 1153, the *qiyāmat,* ''resurrection,'' was announced, which amounted to a complete spiritualization of the Law.

The assassins also played a role during the Crusades: the mysterious *shaikh al-jabal,* ''the Old Man of the Mountain,'' who had his seat in northern Syria, sometimes sent his followers to interfere with the fighting. Alamut was conquered by the Mongols in 1256; the last Syrian fortresses were captured in 1272 by the Egyptian Mamluks.

Some of the Ismailis continued to live in Eastern Iran, others in Syria.

The followers of Musta'li settled mainly in Yemen, where Queen Hurra played an important role in their early history. Their missionaries, *dā'ī*, soon reached Gujarat, where they were followed by missionaries of the Nizaris, who were particularly active in Sind. It is possible that the previous presence of Qarmathians around Multan facilitated their work, for they succeeded in winning a considerable number of followers in Sind and Gujarat by an esoteric transformation of some Hindu ideas. Thus, 'Ali appears as the longed-for tenth *avatar* of Vishnu. Religious songs, *gināns*, often ascribed to the first Pirs, the founders of the Ismaili settlements, were composed in the regional languages (Sindhi, Gujarati, Panjabi etc.); their authors took over the symbolism of the indigenous popular poetry to sing of the soul's love for the *imām*. Most *gināns* were formerly written in a special alphabet, called Khojki (the Nizaris were often called *Khoja*).

The Indian Ismailis used to send their tithe to the *imām* who, after the fall of Alamut, continued to reside in Iran. Due to political reasons the *imām* decided, in 1839, to leave for India. He was known as Aga Khan; and the third Indian leader, the famed Sultan Muhammad Aga Khan III, transformed the Ismaili community during his more than sixty years of leadership, encouraging them to participate in modern economic ventures. Ismailis live not only in Pakistan, Bombay, and the mountains of Hunza and Chitral, but have also emigrated, following the Aga Khan's order, to East Africa. Recent political events forced the members of a well-to-do community to emigrate, and Canada has now one of the largest numbers of Ismailis. Their organization and their emphasis on education are remarkable. According to the late Aga Khan's order, girls should be given a particularly good education. The Aga Khan is the *ḥāżir imām*, the infallible "present" *imām*.

The followers of Musta'li accept *Sayyidnā*, "our Lord," as their spiritual leader, who, however, does not claim the same status as the Aga Khan. The Musta'lians are usually called Bohoras; as this Indian term indicates, they are generally successful merchants in India and Pakistans. One of their sub-divisions boasts the presence of personalities who played an important role in the modernization of Indian Islam, such as A. A. A. Fyzee, whose studies about the work of the Fatimid judge Qadi Nu'man (to this day the basis of Bohora law) and his modern interpretation of Islam are worthy of mention. The first Muslim president of the Indian National Congress, Badraddin Tyabjee, belonged to the Bohoras, as did Atiya Begum, the active woman educationist and friend of Muhammad Iqbal in the first half of this century. One should not forget that M. A. Jinnah, the Quaid-i azam, "the greatest leader" and political architect of Pakistan, was the scion of an Ismaili family. Lately, a more conservative attitude can be seen among the Bohoras, once noted for their progressive stance.

While the last two Ismaili groups are politically and culturally very active in our days, another Shia-based group has fallen into oblivion. These are the Hurufis whose founder, Fadlullah of Astarabad, lived toward the end of the fourteenth century. He combined Shia ideas with cabalistic approaches to the deeper meaning of numbers and letters. Such speculations had been practiced among the mystics from at least the ninth century, but Fadlullah regarded everything in the world as an expression of numbers and letters. Hurufi speculations continued at least in part among Turkish dervishes, especially the Bektashis, who in any case have a strong penchant toward Shia doctrines. Bektashi poetry, written in popular meters in simple Turkish, abounds in eulogies for 'Ali and his family. The names of the *Panjtan,* (the five holy persons: Muhammad, 'Ali, Fatima, Hasan, and Husain) and invocations such as the prayer *Nadi 'Aliyyan* ("Call upon 'Ali the locus of manifestation for wondrous things") are often written in imaginative Arabic calligraphy among the Bektashis. One of the most important representatives of the Hurufi sect was the Turkish poet Nesimi, cruelly killed in Aleppo in 1417. In later times Hurufi tendencies were now and then combined with *jafr,* that is, the secret knowledge possessed by the Prophet's family that enabled them (and their followers) to predict the future by interpreting the letters and the numerical value of Koranic verses.

It is common to all Shiite groups to reject (*tabarra'*) the first three caliphs who, according to ʿAli's faithful adherents, were usurpers, since the caliphate was destined, beyond doubt, for ʿAli. That is why the names of Abu Bakr, ʿUmar, and ʿUthman are not used in Shia nomenclature. The moderate Zaidites refrain from the *tabarra'*. It is this rejection, nay even the cursing of the first three caliphs (who were among the first believers and were honored companions of the Prophet), which constitutes a strong barrier between Sunnites and Shiites. A predilection for ʿAli and the House of the Prophet is also a common attitude among pious Sunnites.

In nineteenth-century Iran a new current appeared, which was based to a certain degree upon the religious school of the Shaikhis. It is Babism, so called because its founder, Muhammad ʿAli of Tabriz, declared himself in 1826 to be the *bāb,* "the gate" through which a believer can enter God's presence. The Babi movement was cruelly persecuted in Iran; the Bab and his faithful disciples were largely killed. Among them was the highly sensitive poetess Tahira Qurrat ul-ʿAin (d. 1852): as the Bab intended to free women from strict veiling, the Babi movement became very attractive for women who hoped to enjoy a new freedom and activity. Babism (which ascribed a special value to the number Nineteen, the numerical value of *wāḥid,* One) emphasizes in the first place the ethical attitude of human beings. Though in the beginning Babism remained by and large within the framework of mystically-tinged Shia Islam, the Bab's successor, Baha Ullah (d. 1892) led the movement in a more radical direction. His followers, the Bahai, claim to stand in the same relation to Islam as Christianity does to Judaism. Islamic law is abolished, and the equality of all humans and general tolerance are promulgated. The repression of the Bahais continues in Iran and elsewhere. As they claim to possess a religion that emerged after the one preached by Muhammad, "the Seal of the prophets," traditional Islamic law cannot tolerate them, lofty as their ideas may be.

Mystical Islam and Sufi Brotherhoods

It is conceivable that the inner life of Islam might have been suffocated in the ever-narrowing net of dogmatic definitions and scholastic methods, or in the external ritual and legal prescriptions which seemed to increase almost year to year. However, a new current, mysticism, appeared in the world of Islam and gave it, in many areas, a special form. This mystical current is called Sufism, a word derived from *ṣūf*, "wool." From this term one can understand the originally ascetic character of the movement, for just as early Christian ascetics in the Near East used to wear woolen cloaks, thus early Muslim ascetics too donned a dark, usually dark blue, woolen garb. To understand the reason for the growth of such a movement, one has to remember that soon after Muhammad's death tension arose between the world-conquering Umayyad rulers and pious believers, who were deeply influenced by the terrible descriptions in the Koran of the Last Judgment and felt the need of incessant repentance. Hasan al-Basri (d. 728), who is quoted by most theological schools as a witness for their opinions, always emphasized the fear of Hell:

> O son of Adam! You will die alone and enter the grave alone and be resurrected alone, and it is with you alone that the reckoning will take place! O son of Adam! It is you who is intended! It is you who is addressed!

In Hasan's environment and probably under his influence, the first-known ascetics of the Iraqi and Syrian lands appeared, men and women who devoted themselves as far as possible to nightly vigils, who extended their fast far beyond the prescribed times, and who carefully avoided not only things prohibited or disapproved of but even those which were permitted but were, in the eyes of sensitive people, perhaps of doubtful merit. They constantly fought against the *nafs,* the lower soul principle that "instigates to evil" (Sura 12/53), for according to a saying of the Prophet, struggle against the *nafs* is "the greatest *jihād,*" the true "Holy War" in the service of God. Unceasing control of each and every thought and action was refined to become a science of its own, so that one's whole life could be led in perfect *ikhlāṣ,* "purity of devotion".

Ascetic movements developed not only in Mesopotamia but even more in Eastern Iran, in Khorasan, where one cannot exclude a certain influence of Buddhist monastic ideals. The first noted ascetic of the East, Ibrahim ibn Adham (d. ca. 777) hailed from Balkh, in the ancient province of Bactria. Although he was the scion of Arab settlers, a central motif of the Buddha legend was transferred to him: he becomes in legends the prince who leaves home to wander into homelessness.

For Ibrahim and his compatriots one of the most important aspects of true religious life was absolute trust in God, *tawakkul,* which, however went far beyond the Prophet's practical advice: "First tie your camel and then trust in God!" For the early Sufis it meant to refrain completely from carrying any money or food when traveling, to refrain also from taking any medical help, or even to refute food that was not directly given to them. Stories of this exaggerated *tawakkul*, which often verge on the grotesque, are plentiful in early hagiographies. For later Sufis, *tawakkul* remained central as an ethical attitude but was not practiced in this overstressed form. One understood that *tawakkul* was basically nothing but the practical aspect of *tauḥīd*: one trusts in God because there is no bestower of goods but Him, and His name *ar-razzāq*, "the One Who nourishes," is a promise that He will care for all the needs of His creatures.

Another central concept in early Sufism is *faqr*, "poverty." The Sufis relied on the Prophet's saying: *Faqrī fakhrī*, "My poverty is my pride." *Faqr* in the first place requires that one renounce any worldly possessions. Such material poverty remained the Sufi ideal for a long time (even though in later centuries many of the "poor" (*faqīr, dervish*) turned into influential landlords and, contrary to the early ascetic ideals, even cooperated with the ruling classes). But as *tawakkul* was interiorized into an ethical ideal, so was poverty: it means to feel poor and destitute in the presence of the Eternally Rich, self sufficient God (cf. Sura 35/16). Nothing really belongs to a human being; the wealth of this world lasts only for a few days. For this reason some Sufis claimed that the spiritual rank of a grateful rich person able to part with all his wealth in a single moment without regret is comparable to that of a poor person who patiently suffers his poverty. The poor, however, who is grateful—even for not receiving anything—is superior to all others, for gratitude, like all other stations on the mystical path, has three stages: thanks for receiving something, thanks for not receiving it, and gratitude for the capacity of being grateful. *Faqr*, however, could be taken in the sense of "giving up every good," and even more "giving up hopes and wishes for the next world." It can become almost a coterminus of *fanā*, "annihilation" (*Entwerden* "de-becoming"). This is the view expressed in the frequently quoted saying that appears first in the twelfth century: "When poverty becomes perfect it is God." That is, the creature in his absolute poverty is lost, so to speak, in the eternally rich Creator who becomes everything for him.

In the uninterrupted struggle against the *nafs*, not only are poverty and fasting, nightly vigils and, often, silence required, but also constant introspection; worse than clinging to worldly goods is haughtiness, complacency, and striving for fame and praise. "The *nafs* has a Koran and a rosary in the one hand and a dagger in the sleeve." Thus says Rumi, pointing to the danger that one may be all too pleased with one's own piety, with one's devotional works, and with one's renown as a "saintly" person. It is better to be outwardly sinful and draw people's anger and blame than to attract praise by a show of piety. This was at least the view of the so-called Malamatiya, a group of intensely pious seekers in the tenth and eleventh centuries, whose sobriquet is derived from *malāma*, "blame." However, as other Sufis objected, even that attitude is far from perfect, for as long as the Sufi cares at all for people's reaction, be it praise or blame, he has not yet reached true insight. The goal is, first of all, *ridā*, "contentment," grateful acceptance of whatever comes. A story from the tenth century tells that a Sufi addressed God in his prayer:

> "O Lord, are you satisfied with me that I am satisfied with Thee?"
>
> He heard a voice: "You liar! if you were satisfied with Me you would not ask whether I am satisfied with you!"

The purely ascetic way of life did not remain a goal in itself. In the middle of the eighth century, the first signs of genuine love mysticism appear among the pious. Its first representative was a woman, Rabi'a of Basra (d. 801). Numerous are the legends that surround this great woman saint of Islam. The following one was famous enough to be taken over into medieval and modern European literature, though without mentioning Rabi'a's name:

> She was seen one day in the streets of Basra, carrying a bucket in one hand and a torch in the other one. Asked the

meaning of her action, she replied: "I want to pour water into Hell and set fire to Paradise so that these two veils disappear and nobody worships God out of fear of Hell or hope for Paradise, but only for the sake of His eternal beauty."

This absolute love, which does not care for Hell and its punishments nor for the pleasures of the paradisial gardens, became central themes, if not *the* central theme, of mystical poetry down to this day.

Most theologians, understandably, refused to use the term "love" for the relation between man and God. Love, they claimed, is love for God's commands, hence, absolute obedience to the Law. Yet the strong element of Love could not be pushed aside. Like Rabi'a, the Sufis liked to refer to Sura 5/59: "He loves them and they love Him." These words, although taken out of context, seem to prove the possibility of mutual love, which—like every act in the world—begins in and from God.

In the century and a half after Rabi'a's death, theories of love were elaborated and enlarged. In her Iraqi homeland a number of mystics continued defining love and other mystical states and stations: One finds in Baghdad a psychologist, Muhasibi (d. 857), named after his tendency to search his soul (*muḥāsaba*) with utter sobriety; and a penetrating spirit such as Kharraz, whose importance for the formulation of the mystical profession of faith was understood only recently. It was this mystic who stated that "Only God has the right to say 'I'." He thus prepared the ground for the extension of the formula of *tauḥīd* into its later form, e.g., "There is nothing existing but God." Muhasibi's contemporary in Egypt was Dhu'n-Nun, of Nubian descent (d. 859). He was surrounded by miracle stories but is also known as the first to define *ma'rifa*, "gnosis, nondiscursive knowledge." Allegedly, he was an alchemist— but what is Sufism but the alchemy of the soul, the transmutation of base matter into pure spiritual gold? Dhu'n-Nun seems to be the first Sufi to rediscover nature as a witness to God's wondrous activities, thus giving creation a certain value, an attitude very different from that of the world-hating ascetics, for whom this world was nothing but a dunghill, no more important than a gnat's wing.

Dhu'n-Nun rightly remembered the Koranic words that everything praises God in its own silent language, and thus he translated nature's songs in his prayers:

> O God, I never hearken to the voices of the beasts or the rustle of the trees, the splashing of the waters or the song of the birds, the whistling of the wind or the rumble of the thunder but I sense in them a testimony to Thy Unity and a proof of Thy incomparability, that Thou art the All-Prevailing, the All-Knowing, the All-True.

Such psalm-like prayers of the Egyptian mystic may have inspired, but are at least echoed in, later mystical poetry, mainly in the Persianate world, whose authors understood the praise of God as uttered by flower, stone, and animal.

Another contemporary of the two just-mentioned Sufis is the Persian Bayezid Bistami (d. 874), whose strange, lonely personality has become almost proverbial. His exclamation *Subḥānī*, "Praise be to me! How great is my Majesty!" has often been interpreted by later Sufis as the expression of man's deification once he has been "annihilated" from the world and from himself. Bayezid's emphasis on *fanā*, "annihilation" as well as some of his paradoxical expressions have been explained by some scholars as influenced by Indian Vedanta speculations. However, he advocates not the expansion of the *atman* until it realizes its oneness with *Brahman* but rather wants to extinguish all traces of human nature. Bayezid was the first to use the symbolism of the heavenly journey when speaking of his raptures and has described his longing for *fanā* in highly poetical images, as well as his inexplicable disappointment at the end of his experiences.

Fanā is in the first place an ethical concept, i.e., the renunciation of human qualities and increasing spiritualization; it has nothing to do with Indian concepts of *nirvana* since it does not mean the attempt to be rescued from the painful cycle of birth and rebirth but rather the return of the creature to the state "as he was before he was."

This latter formulation was coined by one of the most renowned masters of early Sufism, Junaid of Baghdad (d. 910), "the peacock of the poor," through whom all later chains of initiation reach back to the Prophet, either via ʿAli or Abu Bakr. Junaid is regarded as the leading representative of mystical sobriety, in contrast to ecstatic intoxication, and his influence is palpable not only in the Iraqian scene but also in later Sufism, especially in the Maghrib, as well. To be sure, one could also find in Iraq more poetically-minded Sufis who blended love of humanity with love of God but sometimes uttered words that horrified the dogmatic theologians. Junaid was well aware of the danger that lofty ideas of mystical union might be discussed or merely mentioned before the non-initiated, for in his earlier days (877) some lawsuits against the allegedly heretic tendencies of the Sufis had been filed in the capital. He therefore taught his disciples in coded and difficult-to-decipher words and, as legend has it, predicted a terrible end to one of the mystics who preached openly of the interiorization of Islam and its ritual duties.

This disciple, however, was to become the hero of mystical and non-mystical poets, the model of the daring lover who expressed the secret of loving union between man and God (or, as later mystics saw it, spoke of the all-embracing Unity of Being) in his word *ana'l-ḥaqq*, "I am the absolute Truth," that is "I am God." Hallaj, hailing from Persian Iraq and famed for his almost superhuman feats of asceticism, did not actually exclaim this famed sentence at Junaid's door, as legend tells. The quintessence of his doctrine is that Adam was created in the image of the human nature, *nāsūt*, that is inherent in God, and that the uncreated Divine Spirit can overcome the created human spirit in rare moments of ecstasy, although the eternal and that which is created in time are essentially incompatible.

Hallaj wandered through the the eastern lands of the caliphate; around 905 he reached the Indus Valley and then moved on to Inner Asia, probably following the Silk Route. His disciples lived everywhere between Turkestan and Mecca; their last correspondence with him was confiscated by the police when he was finally arrested and imprisoned. However, it was not so much his mystical teaching (which seemed suspect and dangerous even to many other Sufis in Baghdad) that made him suspect in the eyes of the Abbasid government; rather, political moves were at work. He was accused of contracts with the Qarmathians in Multan and of revolutionary conspiracy. Indeed, he called on Muslims to understand their religion not so much according to the letter, but in keeping with the spirit, although this was a dangerous stance. His numerous prayers asked for the "lifting of the veil" between God and himself, and he urged people to kill him so they would be recompensed for a pious action, while he eventually would be freed from the "I" that always stood between him and God, the God who manifests Himself everywhere to those who have eyes to see. His verse:

> Kill me, O my trustworthy friends
> for in my being killed is my life,

inspired numerous mystics and was elaborated in various forms. On March 26, 922, he was cruelly executed. His short poems are the most tender expressions of mystical, non-sensual love that are known in Arabic; in his *Kitāb aṭ-ṭawāsīn* he used for the first time the allegory of the moth that casts itself into the candle's flame—an image that was to become a favorite with later Sufi poets in the Persianate world. It also inspired the German poet Goethe in his moving poem *Selige Sehnsucht*, "Blessed longing."

For later Sufis, Hallaj's death was a model of death through love; his name, but even more his father's name Mansur "victorious" is well-established in the poetry of the eastern Islamic world, while his saying "I am the Truth" is usually translated as "I am God," *ḥaqq*, ("truth, reality") being the favorite mystical term for God. The bold mystic was praised not only by classical and modern Sufis, but his name is a keyword in modern—usually progressive—poetry in the Muslim world, for he sacrificed his life for his ideals and was killed by the establishment.

Only the 'sober' brotherhoods are somewhat critical of him, regarding him as too narrow a vessel for Divine inspiration.

Hallaj's death can be taken in a certain respect as the end of the first, classical period of Sufism, which at that time could be described as "voluntarist mysticism." In subsequent centuries one observes an increasing systematization, a development that was necessary not only because the Sufis had to prove their orthodox stance, but also because of the increase in foreign influences (Neo-platonism, Christianity, and later Central Asian and Indian ascetic techniques). A great number of works in Arabic and, from the mid-eleventh century also in Persian, were composed to prove not only the compatibility of Sufism with Islamic teaching, but rather to show that there was indeed no difference between the two. All early mystics are firmly grounded in the *sharīʿa*, whose rules and commands they took extremely seriously, while at the same time seeking to discover the deeper meaning of the words. For it is the broad road, *sharīʿa*, from which the narrow path, *ṭarīqa*, the path trod by the chosen few, can branch out, and it is the Koran in which every wisdom can be found.

Systematization attained its high point in the *Iḥyāʾ ʿulūm ad-dīn* of Abu Hamid al-Ghazzali (d. 1111), a Persian scholar who, after a very successful career in one of the leading theological colleges of his time, turned to mysticism. His autobiography *Al-munqidh min aḍ-ḍalāl*, ("the savior from error") shows his spiritual wrestling with the various theological currents of his time—philosophy, scholasticism, and Batiniyya. The final leap into Sufism saved him and removed his doubts. His major work, the *Iḥyāʾ ʿulūm ad-dīn*, aims as its title says at the "revivification of the sciences of religion" or, in short, "of theology" in a broad sense; in other words it introduces the believer into a life that is agreeable to God. In addition to *islām*, "absolute surrender," and *īmān*, "faith," one also needs *iḥsān* which means "to serve God as if one were seeing Him." One has to be conscious of God's presence in every moment. This feeling of God's constant presence is valid even while one is busy with most non-religious actions, and for this reason the *Iḥyā'* contains in its first three parts injunctions about correct behavior in every moment, be it marriage or prayer, commerce or travel. Only the fourth part is devoted to more clearly religious and mystical issues such as poverty, patience, trust in God, longing, love, and gnosis; these lead in the fortieth and final chapter to the seeker's attitude at the time of death. This is the aim of the entire book which, thanks to its readable style and logical argumentation, was soon accepted as standard, thus tempering mainstream Islam with a moderately mystical flavor. When reading the *Iḥyā'* one should remember that forty is not only the number of patience and maturity and the number of days that the Sufi has to spend in the *chilla,* seclusion, but also the number of degrees between man and God; furthermore, it is the numerical value of the letter *M,* the abbreviation of Muhammad.

It is amazing, however, that Ghazzali in his booklet *Mishkāt al-anwār,* "the niche for lights" deals with a completely different aspect of Sufism, i.e., the mysticism of illumination, *ishrāq,* a trend that was expressed most lucidly nearly a century later by the brilliant young Suhrawardi, (executed in 1191 and hence called *maqtūl,* "killed"). Suhrawardi's work constitutes an ingenious blending of Greek, Iranian, ancient Near Eastern, and Islamic concepts, and teaches in philosophical Arabic writings and delightful Persian allegories the soul's return from the 'western exile' of matter to the eastern, spiritual world of pure light. As for Abu Hamid al-Ghazzali's younger brother Ahmad, he showed little interest in the ethical problems facing the normal Muslim believer with which his brother had to cope, but he composed the subtlest work on mystical love known in classical Persian literature. It sparked off a series of similar attempts to approach the secret of Divine Love.

Shortly after Abu Hamid al-Ghazzali's death a new period of Sufism set in—that is, the crystallization of brotherhoods and Sufi orders, *ṭarīqa.* Earlier mystics usually gathered around a master in small groups; the master (*shaikh* in Arabic, *pīr* in Persian) or guide (*murshid*) often

had his everyday profession and might be a simple crafts-
man or a learned scholar. It seems that with ʿAbdul Qadir
al-Gilani (Jilani; d. 1166) a process was triggered that was
to change the cultural scene considerably. ʿAbdul Qadir
himself, a Hanbalite preacher in Baghdad, probably never
thought of founding a real Sufi order, but his disciples organized themselves into a brotherhood, while at about the
same time other Sufi teachers also began to attract large
numbers of followers who had to be organized properly. It
has been speculated that the extinction of most Ismaʿili
centers, which seemed to offer the population a certain
spiritual assistance, may have left a void which the orders
were able to fill.

In these groups pious Muslims, who benefited but little from the increasing dogmatism and legalism in official
Islam, could find the kind of emotional religiosity that they
sorely missed. Communal prayers and often musical ses-
sions proved attractive; the shaikh or his substitute, *khalīfa,*
cared for the followers' personal problems, and thus his
house attracted many searching and seeking souls. The *pīr*
had virtually unlimited power over the disciple, *murīd,* who
was initiated by grasping the master's hand and was thus
integrated into the *silsila,* the chain of initiation and suc-
cession which led back to the Prophet. Before the master,
the disciple should be, according to an old saying, "like a
dead body in the hand of the undertaker." The shaikh carefully supervised the spiritual development of the *murīd,*
sent him into the forty days' seclusion, and, most importantly, entrusted him with the right formula of *dhikr.* From
early days onward the Sufis dwelt upon the importance of
the uninterrupted remembrance of God, *dhikr.* They found
support in Koranic sentences which invite humankind to remember God often, and especially in Sura 13/28: "Verily
by remembering God, hearts become calm." The regular
repetition of certain formulas thousands of times was practiced from early days and grew into the central spiritual
technique among the brotherhoods. The *dhikr* can consist of
the word "Allah," the profession of faith, formulas asking
for forgiveness or praising the Lord, or, very important,

one of the Ninety-nine Most Beautiful Names of God. It can be performed aloud or silently. In the meetings of many orders the common performance of the loud *dhikr* is an important means to attain an ecstatic state. Generally, however, the silent *dhikr* is regarded as preferable. Combined with a breathing technique, refined over the centuries, *dhikr* is the central duty of the *murīd,* while the master's duty is to give the disciple the *dhikr* that is appropriate for his mental stage; for the Divine Names, when repeated thousands of times, can lead to dangerous psychological and even physiological consequences.

Due to the rapid spread of the orders, Sufism increasingly grew into a mass movement which came to embrace, beyond the true disciples, numerous loosely affiliated members and 'friends' (comparable to the Third Orders or lay members of an order in the Catholic church). Most of them would attend the *ʿurs,* the celebration during the anniversary of the founder's death ("wedding," "spiritual nuptials," for the saint's soul was united with God on this day). During the *ʿurs* they would pray together, share special food, and celebrate in various ways that were not always strictly religious. Thanks to the orders' activities, the religious contents of Islam, especially love of God, love of His Prophet, and love of His creatures, reached large parts of the population who otherwise would barely have come in touch with official theology and would probably not have understood it in any case.

The model of the Qadiriyya, based on ʿAbdul Qadir Jilani, was followed by many others, but to this day the Qadiriyya's members are found in considerable numbers from West Africa to Indonesia. That the founder himself had forty-nine sons proves that celibacy was by no means required in Sufism; one would rather follow the Prophet's model in getting married. One member of the Qadiriyya was the Mughal heir apparent, Dara Shikoh (executed in 1659), who translated fifty Upanishads into Persian and dreamt and wrote about the "meeting of the two oceans" (Sura 18/65), that is, Islam and Hinduism, on the basis of mysticism. The Rifaʿiyya (who trace themselves back to

Ahmad ar-Rifaʿi, d. 1183) are generally known as Howling
Dervishes because their loud *dhikr* causes a harsh, almost
frightening sound; they are noted for strange 'miracles'
such as wounding themselves, taking out their eyes, eating
glass or live snakes, and other feats which, according to
reliable hagiographers, was not what the founder had intended. Around 1200 the Suhrawardiyya became prominent; their roots go back to Abu Najib as-Suhrawardi
(d. 1153) and his nephew, who also served as the caliph's
spiritual ambassador. It is a highly cultured 'sober' order
which was successful in India (Baha'uddin Zakariya of
Multan, d. 1266) as far as Bengal. Contrary to other major
orders, especially the Chishtiyya, the Suhrawardiyya
followed their second founder's example and dealt actively
with politics. In this respect they resemble the Central
Asian Naqshbandiyya, who wielded enormous political
power in Central Asia in the fifteenth century and later
counteracted "intoxicated" Sufism and what seemed to
their trends sullying the purity of faith. The Naqshbandis,
famed for their silent *dhikr,* extended their influence especially to India and Turkey.

   In Central Asia the Kubrawiyya appeared. Their
founder, Najmuddin Kubra, offered psychologically highly
interesting interpretations of the color visions experienced
by some Sufis on the path. In Egypt the order of Ahmad
al-Badawi (d. 1278) (which has preserved several pre-
Islamic elements) remained restricted to the Nile Valley; its
festive days are regulated according to the solar, not the lunar, year and to the rise of the Nile. Again in Egypt and
about the same time, the Shadhiliyya appeared and took
over many traditions of the sober Baghdadi school. Its
modern derivations in North Africa have lately attracted
a number of Europeans and Americans. The Shadhiliyya
literature boasts the Arabic *Ḥikam* by Ibn ʿAta Allah
(d. 1309), brief but supremely beautiful Arabic words of
wisdom:

> A sign that God has placed you at some place is that He
> makes you stay there and you give good fruit.

The protective prayer composed by the founder of the *ṭarīqa*, the *ḥizb al-baḥr*, was well-known as a strong protecting talisman even in India.

In Anatolia, the Mevleviyya grew, inspired by Jalaluddin Rumi (d. 1273) and organized by his son; they are known in the West as the Whirling Dervishes because of their whirling dance (the only institutionalized musical *dhikr* in the Muslim world). But while the Mevleviyya in the Ottoman Empire attracted primarily members of court circles and artists, another brotherhood in Anatolia, the Bektashiyya, adopted a good number of Shiite elements and was the religious mainstay of the Janissaries, the elite troops of the Ottomans. The simple but often powerful Bektashi lyrical poetry is remarkable. But the Bektashis were frequently accused of libertinism because they allowed women to participate freely in their meetings. When the Janissaries were uprooted in 1826, the Bektashis too lost their power outwardly, yet Bektashi jokes are still alive in Turkey.

Mevleviyya and Bektashiyya never crossed the borders of the Ottoman Empire (which included the Balkans), while in India the Chishtiyya too remained restricted to the subcontinent. Their founder Muʿinuddin Chishti (d. 1236) came out of the Suhrawardi tradition, and from his seat in Ajmer, Rajasthan, the order soon spread to Delhi and to southern India. It continues to be one of the most active *ṭarīqas* in India. Like the Mevlevis, the Chishtis too excel in music and are noted for their love of poetry. The role of these orders in the process of conversion in the fringe areas of Islam cannot be overrated.

The thirteenth century was the high time of Sufism, despite the disaster caused by the Mongol onslaught, which completely changed the political landscape of the central and eastern lands of Islam; or perhaps Sufism was an antidote to the destruction in the material world. The *magister magnus* of later Sufism, the Spanish-born Ibn ʿArabi (d. 1240), was inspired in Mecca to compose his enormous work, the *Futūḥāt al-makkiyya*, "the Meccan revelations." His thought was to dominate the entire mystical

literature in subsequent centuries, and even those who did
not accept his concept of *waḥdat al-wujūd*, "Unity of Being" (a term he himself never used) could not avoid his influence in both language and thought.

Ibn ʿArabi has been called a pantheist by many of his
critics in East and West, but his modern interpreters are
able to prove that he always maintained God's transcen-
dence. God's essence in its Unicity remains unknowable
and is beyond everything imaginable; He manifests Himself
through His Names and Attributes and sees Himself in the
mirror He created—that is, the world. Ibn ʿArabi, like
many of his predecessors, repeatedly quoted the famous Divine extra-Koranic word, *ḥadīth qudsī:* "I was a hidden treasure and wanted to be known, thus I created the world."
The world exists only insofar as it is dependent upon God,
and therefore Ibn ʿArabi can say: We ourselves are the attributes by which we describe God; our existence is an
objectivation of His existence; God is necessary for us in
order to exist while we are necessary for Him in order to
manifest Himself. Ibn ʿArabi has laid down his ideas in numerous books and treatises. The *Futūḥāt al-makkiyya* with
its 560 chapters is his most comprehensive work, while the
quintessence of his prophetology is found in the *Fuṣūs
al-ḥikam*, the "bezels of wisdom." In this comparatively
small book, inspired as he claims by the Prophet himself,
he deals in twenty-seven chapters with a mystical prophetology culminating in Muhammad, the Perfect Man in
whom the pleroma of Divine manifestations becomes visible; he is the first thing ever created, the archetype of
humanity. The roots of such ideas are found in early
Sufism, such as Hallaj's prophetology. But with Ibn ʿArabi,
Sufism becomes *ʿirfān*, a kind of special mystical knowledge, and does not necessarily maintain its personal volun-
taristic character; this change has been considered by
critics in both East and West as one of the reasons for the
'stagnation' of Islam after the thirteenth century.

Ibn ʿArabi's ingenious visionary systematization
(which always rests upon the Koran) apparently answered
all metaphysical questions and was gladly accepted by his

contemporaries and followers. In contrast, the works of Jalaluddin Rumi, junior to Ibn 'Arabi by half a century, became a treasure trove of mystically inspired poetry. Except for short, sometimes delightful verses, the Arab world had produced but little mystical poetry in the early period of Sufism. Ibn 'Arabi himself composed a collection of love poems, and during his time the small collection of Arabic odes by the Egyptian Ibn al-Farid (d. 1235) is remarkable for its beauty. The Egyptian poet has sung of the mystery of Divine Love in the highly refined style of classical Arabic love poetry; his *Tā'iyyat al-kubrā* describes man's way to God in more than 750 verses and fascinating images.

Yet the real homeland of mystical poetry was Iran. After the great mystic 'Abdullah-i Ansari (d. 1089 in Herat) wrote his short prayers, interspersed with heartfelt little verses, another poet, again in the easternmost part of Iran (today's Afghanistan), made an even more important contribution to the development of mystical poetry: this was Sana'i of Ghazna (d. 1131), the first to use the form of *mathnawī*, "rhyming couplets," to create a didactic poem about themes known among the Sufis. His *Ḥadīqat al-ḥaqīqa*, "the orchard of truth," is certainly not written in ecstatic rapture, but its form and contents—the combination of anecdotes and their application to Sufi life—have influenced all later Sufi writers. As a lyrical poet Sana'i wrote deeply felt religious poems with breathtaking rhetorical art. His tradition was continued by Fariduddin 'Attar (d. 1220 in Nishapur) who can be considered the master epico-mystical poet of Iran. His vast knowledge of Sufism is evident from his *Tadhkirat al-auliyā*, a romantically embellished hagiographical work, and his talent as a story teller becomes clear from his epics, among which the *Manṭiq aṭ-ṭair*, "the birds' conversation" (based on Sura 27/16) is most famous. The poet describes the journey of the soul birds in quest of their king, the Simurgh. After thirty birds have wandered through the seven valleys on the long and hard path, they reach the Simurgh's place and finally realize that they themselves, being thirty birds—that is, in Persian, *sī murgh*—are identical with the *Sīmurgh:* the individual soul is identical with the Divine Soul. In another epic poem, *Muṣībatnāma,* "the book of affliction," ʿAttar projects in poetical myths the different spiritual stages of the *murīd* during the forty days' seclusion: the seeker asks wind and sun, angels and beasts the way to God, and their answers are interpreted by the master; in the end, the seeker finds God in the "ocean of his soul."

It is told that ʿAttar, shortly before his death, had blessed Jalaluddin Rumi who, born in 1207 north of Balkh, Afghanistan, fled along with his father, a mystical theologian, and his family. Whether or not his father, Baha'uddin Walad, left home for political or other reasons is not known. After long peregrinations the family eventually reached Asia Minor or Rum (hence Jalaluddin's surname *Rūmī*), and Baha'uddin spent the last three years of his life (he died in 1231) in Konya, the ancient Iconium, where the court of the Rum Seljukids attracted refugees, scholars, and artists fleeing from the Mongols. After his father's death Jalaluddin was initiated into the mystical tradition by a disciple of his father and he experienced mystical love when he met, in 1244, Shamsuddin of Tabriz, a wandering dervish of about Rumi's age. Shams introduced him to the heights of Divine Love; he himself claimed to have reached the rank of "the beloved." Shams had to flee from Konya because Jalaluddin's family and disciples strongly disapproved of his close relationship with him; he was brought back after more than a year but disappeared forever in December 1248—assassinated by a jealous group in Rumi's environment. The pangs of longing—already apparent during the first period of separation—transformed Maulana ("our master," Turkish *Mevlâna*) into a poet. More than 35,000 lyrical verses were triggered off by this unique meeting of two mature mystics. After their complete identification, Rumi signed his poems not with his own but with his mystical friend's name. The so-called *Diwan-i Shams* contains probably the most ecstatic verses ever written in Persian; born out of music and whirling dance these poems are notable for their strong rhythm. Their symbols and images are taken from all walks of life, and Maulana's poetry not only transports the reader or listener into the loftiest spheres of ecstasy and love, but also offers a picture of daily life in a medieval Anatolian town.

After Shamsuddin's disappearance Maulana found some consolation in his friendship with Salahuddin Zarkub, a simple but spiritually advanced goldsmith, and finally turned to his disciple Husamuddin Chelebi, at whose behest he composed the nearly 26,000 verses of a mystical didactic poem, *The Mathnawi*. Written in a memorable meter, *The Mathnawi* can be called an encyclopedia of all the mystical ideas and thoughts known in the thirteenth century—it is "the shop of Unity," but equally a treasure house of popular tales and stories. It is, however, not at all a systematic handbook of mystical dogmatics or a well-organized description of esoteric teachings or psychological techniques. Rumi also wrote letters and a prose work and participated in lively social activity along with teaching. After his death in 1273 his *Mathnawi*, called by later admirers "the Koran in the Persian tongue," became the standard mystical work in the Persianate world; numerous commentaries and translations into Turkish and the regional languages of Muslim India were produced through the centuries, and to this day there is barely a poet in the eastern areas of the Islamic world who has not been influenced in some way by Rumi's poetry.

The later history of Iran and Turkey is filled with the names of mystical poets; one may single out that of Fakhruddin ʿIraqi (d. 1289), a delightful Persian poet who lived during Rumi's day in Multan at Baha'uddin Zakariya's place and then stayed some time in Anatolia before turning to Damascus where he is buried not far from Ibn ʿArabi. Later, the most important name is that of Molla Jami (d. 1492 in Herat), poet, mystic, interpreter of classical works, and historian of Sufism. In fact, the role of Sufism for the development of literature in the various languages of the Islamic world cannot be overstated. The Turkish poetry of Yunus Emre (d. 1321) and his followers belongs here, as does early Urdu verse in the Deccan. Sindhi and Panjabi as well as Bengali are replete with mystical

songs, and one can safely say that the popular mystical literature of the Pakistani provinces contains some of the finest products of religious poetry in Islam—whether one
thinks of the powerful, passionate language of Bullhe Shah
in the Punjab (d. 1754), the musical, heart-rending verses
of his contemporary Shah ʿAbdul Latif in Sind (d. 1752),
the ecstatic Sindhi verses by Sachal Sarmast (d. 1826), or
the sonorous, strong lyrics of the Pathan mystic Rahman
Baba (d. ca. 1707). Many unknown treasures can be discovered in this area, and the cross-relations between Indian
Sufi poetry and Hindu *bhakti* poetry have barely been
examined.

Part of this mystical poetry is devoted to the glorifi-
cation of the Prophet. He whom the Koran had called only
a human who had been granted revelation was elevated into
higher spiritual spheres early in Islam; later, the mystics,
following Ibn ʿArabi's example, embellished him with increasingly lofty attributes and invented ever new forms of
praise. In Arabic, Busiri (d. 1297) and his *Burda*, a poem in
honor of Muhammad and the healing power of his Yemeni
cloak, is a good example of this veneration. In Persian and
the other Islamic languages including Hausa and Swahili,
songs in praise of "the best of mankind" were composed
through the ages. To the singer of folksongs he appears
mainly as the intercessor at Doomsday, as God's beloved to
whom one can turn full of trust because God will not refuse
His friend's intercession for his community. He is the
longed-for bridegroom or, as in some Tamil songs, even a
darling child—thus he is ubiquitous although sometimes
appearing in strange garb. Such poems help the Islamicist
understand the immense influence the Sufis exerted upon
the masses, far from the world of speculative theologians
and hairsplitting jurists. Likewise, Sufi influence is evident
in the traditional behavior of Muslims, based on the etiquette described in the *ḥadīth* and refined by the Sufis, an
etiquette derived from the Prophet's noble example and the
model set by his successors. These well-delineated rules of
proper behavior were fundamental in the development of relations between people of different spheres and determined

the social network in countries from Morocco to Indonesia for centuries. It would not be an exaggeration to say that the influence of Islamic mysticism extends from the highest metaphysical speculations to the world of illiterate village women and that it colored large areas of Muslim society before the advent of modern civilization.

Popular Piety and the
Veneration of Saints

Islam, a religion which in theory does not accept any mediator between man and God, underwent a considerable change in the course of the centuries as a veritable cult of saints developed. It is typical of the situation that the stern Hanbalite *madhhab* and, following its lead, the Wahhabis are dead set against Sufism and, as its excrescence, the veneration of saints, although ironically two of the most venerated saints emerged from among the Hanbalites—ʿAbdul Qadir Jilani and ʿAbdullah-i Ansari.

The first systematic treatises about the hierarchy of saints, which culminates in the *quṭb*, the "pole" or "axis," were composed as early as the late ninth century and constitute the basis for later theories. The saint is the *walī*, the "friend of God," who enjoys His special protection. He is blessed with the capacity of performing miracles, but his miracles are called *karāmāt* "charismata," and are of a lower rank than those performed by prophets, which are called *muʿjiza* and serve to confirm the truth of a prophet's message. The mystical teacher, the shaikh, was often elevated to the rank of a saint by his followers and regarded frequently as the *quṭb*, the axis of his time, around whom everything revolves. Absolute obedience to the master is part and parcel of the basic rules of Sufi life from earliest times on, so that it was said: "If someone has no shaikh, Satan is his master."

There is no doubt that a careful and caring spiritual guidance is necessary and required for the disciple, but its later development—the master's absolute authority over his (often poor and illiterate) disciples—can prove very dangerous due to its possible misuse. Modernist critics such as Iqbal see one of the greatest dangers for the Muslim world in what they label with the derogatory term "Pirism". While there is no doubt that some blessed, charismatic leaders of souls exist, a good number of so-called Pirs are prone to attract people and deceive them by skillfully utilizing certain occult powers which are often a result of mystical training or by indulging in highfalutin expressions and mystical-sounding phrases. When one has experienced the behavior of some of these 'Pirs,' one understands better why Ataturk, in 1925, closed the dervish lodges and prohibited all Sufi activity in Turkey, as he wanted to stop the pernicious influence of alleged saints upon the deeply religious people of Anatolia. Nevertheless, the political role of modern Pirs is remarkable; they are sometimes influential in home politics (their followers can be brought to vote for the candidate of their choice), or else they fight the established forms of government. Leaders of some Sufi brotherhoods in the former USSR have countered the dominant political forces and helped to resist russification and irreligiosity in Uzbekistan, the Caucasus, and part of Inner Asia.

The cult of saints is permeated with pre-Islamic ideas (as in other religions as well, where leftovers from previous religions are integrated into the 'high' religion). Ancient local deities survived in saints whose actual names are sometimes unknown and whose tombs are surrounded by legends. Several Christian places and figures are regarded as holy by Muslims as well, e.g., Khidr, St. George, and Elijah. As in Christian saint worship, many saints specialize in curing specific ailments or help in particular cases, be it barrenness, examinations, snakebite, or madness. People come to their tombs to make vows and bring votive offerings. Many of the saints' tombs are located close to springs, caves, or mighty trees; often small patches of cloth are tied at their gates, the trees surrounding the building, or the window grills, to remind the saint of the visitor's request. All kinds of vows are made: one brings brooms to the city saint of Ankara, Hajji Bayram, instead of the former custom of sweeping the saint's threshhold; one sacrifices a sheep; one lights candles; one vows fasting days or a certain number of prayers or recitation from the Koran. The student may say: "If I pass my exam I'll recite Sura *Yāsīn* forty times." And the barren woman may promise to call her son after the saint if her wish is granted (hence the numerous men named *Ghauthbakhsh*, "gift of the help" or *Ghulām-i Dastgīr*, "servant of him who takes by the hand," both surnames of ʿAbdul Qadir Jilani to whose intercession the child is 'owed'.)

A very fertile ground for saint worship is North Africa with its long pre-Islamic past. The same is true in India where some ancient Hindu sanctuaries have been transformed into Muslim shrines; and there is no lack of sacred places such as Ajmir in Rajasthan or Sehwan in Sind, not to mention less famous tombs, where Hindu and Muslim participate together in the cult of a Muslim saint. Every form of sanctuary exists in the subcontinent, from the tank with sacred crocodiles near Karachi to the noble, quiet marble mausoleums in exquisite Mughal architecture, from a simple cell or cave in a rock to a palace-like structure in the teeming bazaar.

Many customs that are practiced near saints' tombs border on magic, and it is indeed one of the shaikh's duties to produce amulets of sorts. One has amulets (incidentally, our word "amulet" is derived from Arabic *hamā'il*) for this or that illness, problems during pregnancy and delivery, danger of fire or theft, and so on. Certain verses of the

Koran have a special power; the recitation of this or that prayer formula protects form danger. A miniature Koran or a golden locket with the name of God, an agate ring or pendant with the Throne Verse, the profession of faith, or (in Shia circles) the names of the *Panjtan* (Muhammad, ʿAli, Fatima, Hasan, and Husain) are often worn as protective charms. In case of illness one may recite the *Fātiḥa* and breathe over the ailing person. Against the evil eye blue beads are used; one can stitch them in a child's garment, hang them somewhere in the car or the bus, or hide them skillfully in a corner of a fine carpet or a precious kelim. Fumigation with rue seed is also common to avert the evil eye.

Even a cult of relics has developed. The Prophet's hairs were coveted objects from very early times as they carried his blessing power; a few years ago the theft of such a hair in Srinagar (Kashmir) resulted in serious riots. The Prophet's gown, *khirqa-i sharīf,* can be admired in Istanbul as well as in Qandahar, Afghanistan. Footprints of the Prophet or of ʿAli—enormous traces in large stones—are displayed in several places. The establishment around a saint's tomb usually owns some objects (a turban, a rosary) that once belonged to the saint or another important personality; in the case of modern saints there may also be more intimate objects (e.g., dentures).

The life of the average Muslim used to follow exactly transmitted rules of behavior and traditional forms. One of the most important moments is the naming of children. Usually the child was given a religious name during the cutting of the umbilical cord. When the ʿaqīqa, the first haircut on the sixth or seventh day was celebrated, the profession of faith was whispered into one of the child's ears and its name into the other ear; also a lamb or goat without blemish was sacrificed.

Among the names given to male children Muhammad takes pride of place, for according to a *ḥadīth* every man called thus will enter Paradise. But in order to avoid desacralization of this name, one often vocalizes its consonants slightly differently—Mihammad or, best known, the Turkish Mehmed. One can also use other names of the Prophet, such as Ahmad or Mustafa, "the Chosen," which partake in the blessing power of the name Muhammad. One frequently finds names composed of the word *ʿabd*, "servant, slave" with one of the Ninety-nine Most Beautiful Divine Names, from ʿAbdullah to ʿAbdul Karim, "servant of the Kind" or ʿAbdul Jabbar, "servant of the Overpowering." All the ninety-nine names can be used in such combinations, although one generally choses the "Names of Grace" that express God's mercy and lovingkindness. For women, *ʿabd* is replaced by *amat*, "maid servant": Amat al-Wadūd, "maid of the Loving." Often the child is named after an ancestor or relative, in particular the grandfather or grandmother. From the later Middle Ages, there was increased use of names composed with *ad-dīn*, "of the religion," (first used only as titles), such as Nasir ad-din, "helper of religion," or Zain-ad-din, "decoration of religion" etc. In the eastern areas of the Islamic world Arabic names become so transformed that they are often incomprehensible to Arabs, because very few parents are acquainted enough with Arabic grammar to understand the true meaning. Such strange constructs might appear when one tries to find an appropriate name for the child by opening the Koran to choose the first meaningful word, e.g., *Uzlifat*, "[Paradise] is brought near" (Sura 81/13). The first letter of a word on a page of the Koran can also be taken as the initial letter of a personal name. Among the Shiites one frequently uses names connected with the Prophet's family—names which, incidentally, are also common among Sunnis. ʿAli, Hasan, Husain, Jaʿfar or combinations with these names are widespread in both major branches of Islam. Although in strict theological terms the word *ʿabd*, "servant," should be used only in connection with a Divine Name, one finds ʿAbd ar-Rasul, "slave of the Prophet," or combinations of *ʿabd* with the name of a Shia *imām*. In such cases many people feel that it is more proper to use the Arabic *ghulām*, "servant," or the Turkish *qul, qūlī* "slave": Ghulam Husain, Ghulam Sayyidain, "slave of the two lords," i.e., Hasan and Husain, or

'Aliquli, "'Ali's slave." Among women, Fatima and her nicknames, such as Zahra, "the radiant," or Batul, "virgin," are common. 'A'isha's name is taboo among Shiites, as are the names of the first three caliphs.

One can express one's special relationship with a saint: Ghulam Rabbani, "servant of the Divinely [inspired master]," i.e., Ahmad Sirhindi. In Turkey, one finds names like Satilmish, "sold," when the parents have vowed that the future child would be "sold," i.e., given to a certain shrine.

One can use names to express one's political and religious ideals, as is done in the West, and it has even happened that a Shiite mother called her son with the highly disliked name Omar because she was utterly charmed by Omar Sharif. Similarly, names tell of the parents' infatuation with this or that political leader or a party program, or with sports' heroes. Lately, a return to properly Islamic names can be observed, especially in Egypt and Iran.

Modern Developments
Inside Islam

At an early time in history, Muslim thinkers asked themselves how Islam could be accommodated to the constantly changing political and social realities, and how one might be able to prevent it from becoming reified and fossilized into an unchangeable pattern of life with an immutable legal system. After the Mongol onslaught and the abolition of the Abbasid caliphate in 1258 had largely destroyed the inherited political forms, there arose a theologian of the stern Hanbalite persuasion, Ibn Taimiyya (d. 1328), who energetically turned against the non-Islamic accretions to popular Sufism and the veneration of saints. He also turned against the lack of true depth in Muslim religious life. Ibn Taimiyya accepted only the Koran and *ḥadīth* as sources of the law and claimed for himself the right of *ijtihād*, that is, the independent, fresh interpretation of these two sources without resorting to the judgments of any of the established religious *madhhabs*. Due to his uncompromising attitude he was imprisoned several times, and yet he was to become the role model for many Muslim modernists who strove for a new interpretation of Islam in the eighteenth and nineteenth centuries. It was at that time that reformers first appeared in various countries—reformers who observed the spiritual as well as political situation of the Muslims with increasing apprehension.

The best known among these reformers is Muhammad ibn ʿ Abdul Wahhab in the Arabian pensinsula, after whom a number of fundamentalist currents in the Islamic worlds were called "Wahhabi." However, Ibn ʿAbdul Wahhab's partisans called themselves *muwaḥḥidūn*, "those who proclaim Divine Unity," true monotheists. Supported by the Arab family of Al Saʿud, they conquered Mecca and Medina in 1803–1806. There they abolished all traces of saint worship and veneration of tombs, including that of the Prophet's mausoleum. Egyptian troops had a difficult time overcoming them and re-establishing their own rule in the holy cities. But a century later, after World War I, when the Saʿud family rose to power in Central Arabia, the Wahhabis gained new strength, and their doctrine spread over the whole area of what was thereafter called Saudi Arabia. Faithful to the Hanbali tradition, they disregard all sources of law and faith except the Koran and *ḥadīth* and interpret these as the only valid foundations of Islamic life.

At about the time of Ibn ʿAbdul Wahhab, Indian theologians too studied in Mecca. The towering figure among them was Shah Waliullah of Delhi (d. 1762), scion of a noted family of theologians. After his return from the pilgrimage he tried to introduce north Indian Muslims into the true meaning of the Koran, which was now, as it seemed to him, obfuscated by and hidden under numerous commentaries and supercommentaries—philosophical, philological, and mystical interpretations that had been composed through the ages. According to his view, one of the reasons for the Muslims's political weakness was their inability to comprehend the meaning of the sacred Book's "clear Arabic language." To facilitate such an understanding, Shah Waliullah translated the Koran into Persian, the language of the educated classes in India. His sons were to do the same with Urdu, the *lingua franca* of the subcontinent. Shah Waliullah was deeply steeped in the mystical tradition, and yet he relentlessly fought against saint worship; but he saw himself graced by visions as "the vicegerent of the Prophet in blaming." His main work in Arabic, *Ḥujjat Allāh al-bāligha,* "God's perfect proof," tried for the first time to explain the Indian Muslims' weakness and decadence as the result of political and social factors and thus inaugurated a new period of Islamic thought. The *Ḥujjat,* written in a quite idiosyncratic Arabic style, is one of the standard works prescribed for students in the Al-Azhar in Cairo, the center of Sunni theology and jurisprudence.

At the same time Waliullah's compatriot in Delhi, the mystical poet Mir Dard (d. 1785) represented the *ṭarīqa muḥammadiyya,* "the Muhammadan Path," which had been founded by his father. The *ṭarīqa muḥammadiyya* is a mystically interiorized fundamentalist movement which half a century later inspired both the name and ideals of a group of Indian Muslim freedom fighters (among them Shah Waliullah's descendant) in the northwest of the subcontinent. The name of the *ṭarīqa* points to the central role of the Prophet in the life and theology of its adherents.

The strong bond with the Prophet is visible also in other currents that surface in the second half of the eighteenth century. It was the Prophet's example that led the members of these *ṭarīqas* to participate actively in the public sector, because the Prophet was not only a religious leader but also a statesman and a practical, pragmatic politician. The two most important groups of this kind were the Tijaniyya, based in Algiers but spreading soon in the central Arabic countries and the Sudan, and the Sanusiyya, mainly in North and Central Africa. The Tijaniyya inspired also the mystico-political movement in Senegal and Hausaland, which finally led to the foundation of the kingdom of Sokoto under the leadership of Osman dan Fodio in 1802. This movement strengthened Islam in West Africa, where a somewhat superficial Islamization had started as early as the twelfth century.

During the eighteenth century the presence of European powers grew stronger in the Islamic world. This was particularly true for India. In retrospect it seems amazing that Shah Waliullah apparently overlooked or was not even aware of the danger that threatened the Delhi kingdom from Bengal, while he tried to secure the help of the neighboring countries, especially Iran, to fight the rising Sikhs and Mahrattas in Central India and the Punjab. Bengal had become a vantage point for the British who, after their victory in the battle of Plassey (1757), slowly but continuously moved westward. The expanding British rule led to difficulties for the Muslims: due to the new revenue regulations, which contradicted Islamic law, an important part of the *auqāf* land was taxed. These pious endowments (*waqf*, plural *auqāf*) are tax-exempt under Islamic law. Their income paid for the upkeep of most mosques and theological colleges along with the professors' and administrators' salaries and facilities for poor students. This change in taxation led, in the course of time, to a deterioration of the traditional educational system in the subcontinent, hence to increasing frustration among the Muslim pious. Other British laws too conflicted with Islamic law and negatively affected the Muslim population. For this reason, one of Shah Waliullah's sons declared that the part of India under British administration was *dār al-ḥarb,* "war country," i.e., non-Muslim. Somewhat later, in 1835, the Macauley edict substituted English for Persian as the official language of administration. Most traditional Muslims refrained from sending their sons to British missionary schools and therefore excluded themselves, as it were, from public service, since they lacked the modern western education required for government servants. Only a slim minority of Muslims attended institutions like Delhi College. It is natural that this situation should have resulted in a steadily growing discontent which eventually triggered the so-called Mutiny, the military revolt of Indian troops, in 1857. The British Crown, blaming the Muslims for the rebellion, took over the administration of major parts of India. The last Mughal ruler, a fine poet and calligrapher, was deposed. He died in exile in Rangoon in 1861, aged nearly ninety.

In other parts of the Muslim world as in India, colonial rule resulted in the formation of new elites, a process in which Muslims usually were relegated to the background, for they were often regarded as the leaders and instigators of rebellion against the new rulers. As W. W. Hunter asks in the title of his book: *Our Indian Muslims— Are they bound in conscience to rebel against the Queen?*

As for Egypt, it was the target in 1798 of Napoleon's expedition, which resulted in the first scholarly investigation of the country and its civilizations, beginning with pharaonic times. It also opened the way for young Muslims to become acquainted with French civilization. However, in the course of the nineteenth century a most unfortunate financial policy again allowed Great Britain to exert the greatest political influence upon the country, which was also important for the passage to India. In 1882, the Khidiw, the Egyptian ruler who wielded barely any power, was placed under the control of Lord Cromer.

In Syria, political trouble flared up, and as early as 1842 the administration of the Lebanese areas was divided on the basis of religious majorities—the consequences of this partition have lasted to this day.

In North Africa, the French occupied vast areas, and the Italians took possession of Cyrenaica, much against the resistance of the Sanusiyya. The Ottoman Empire lost parts of its European provinces due to the Greek rebellion of 1821; other fringe areas also seceded. The Ottoman sultan therefore called to his country German military advisers to assist in his attempts at reforming the army.

In Iran too, the situation became critical when Russian troops invaded the northwestern border areas in 1828, conquering even Ardabil, the sacred place where the Safavid dynasty had its roots. From that moment to the partition of Iran under two spheres of influence, British and Russian, the country went through many crises. In the 1850's, the Leshghian Sufi leader Shamil with his companions in the Caucasus tried to fight the advancing Russians.

Due to changes in the political landscape, more or less intense attempts at reform emerged in almost every part of the Muslim world, for the Muslims craved a way to survive the overwhelming presence of western civilization and preserve their own values without losing touch with modern civilization. In this connection one usually thinks first of a current called *salafiyya,* that is, scholars who aimed at returning to the life and thought of the *salaf,* that is, the earliest generations of Muslims, the true "fathers" of Islamic piety. The *salafiyya* took up Ibn Taimiyya's viewpoint by declaring the Koran and *hadīth* the only valid sources of Muslim life, sources which, however, had to be interpreted anew as time passed. The great pan-Islamic propagandist Jamaluddin Afghani (d. 1897) inspired many a thinker; his ideas were taken up especially in Egypt and were elaborated by Muhammad ʿAbduh (d. 1905) and his disciple Muhammad Rashid Rida (d. 1935). Both of them defended the opinion that the systems of *madhhab,* legal schools which cling to decisions that were fixed by *ijmāʿ* in the Middle Ages were completely outdated, and that every jurist should be allowed to exercise *ijtihād,* free investigation of the two sources. The journal *Manār* in Cairo was the voice of ʿAbduh and Rashid Rida; hence they and their followers are called the Manar Group. Their message was that Islam could be accommodated to the new civilization's challenge without difficulty, that all problems could be solved by applying a new interpretation of the Koran and *hadīth.* Those who follow this line—not only in Egypt but in other countries as well—have striven with more or less skill and certainly with great enthusiasm to find in the Koran evidence pointing to modern developments and scientific discoveries, including even the hydrogen bomb. Understandably, their pride of discovery sometimes makes them exaggerate their 'modern, scientific interpretation.'

India was a particularly fertile soil for modernist ideas. Reacting against the British missionary activities, theologians and writers tried to prove that Islam was not, as the missionaries claimed, a retrogressive religion but was absolutely compatible with the modern world. Did not

Lord Cromer claim that "reformed Islam is no longer Islam"? One had to react against such remarks which were also reflected in the nineteenth-century biographies of the Prophet! The spokesman for the most active modernist current was Sir Sayyid Ahmad Khan (d. 1898) whose views were, it is true, vehemently refuted by Jamaluddin Afghani and who was scolded by many pious Muslim as *nēcharī*, a "naturalist." His great achievement is the foundation of the Anglo-Muslim College in Aligarh (1875), which later was to grow into a university and become one of the centers of modernist ideas. Anglophile as he was, Sir Sayyid admonished the Muslims not to participate in the activities of the Indian National Congress, founded in 1885 as the first political representation of Indians. He was afraid that Muslims would always remain a minority in a parliament elected according to democratic rules and would always be outvoted by the Hindu majority. In such concerns one sees already the roots of the partition of the subcontinent in 1947. The Aligarh movement, mainly interested in the education of the Urdu-speaking upper middle class, was sharply criticized by its antagonist, the school of Deoband, which was founded on the premises of *salafi*-Sufi traditions. The Deobandis were anti-British and later fought against the partition of the subcontinent.

In the latter decades of the nineteenth century, literary works were composed in India which sing of the past glory of Islam (a similar pattern can be seen in Turkey) and Urdu novels were written in the attempt to defend the necessity of reforms. The need for a new way of educating girls and women forms one of the central topics of this literature.

Sir Sayyid left a good number of books and articles in Urdu. His ideas led to the foundation of institutions along the lines of Aligarh in Bengal and in Sind; they also reached the Nizam's Hyderabad, which was, after Delhi, the second center of Islamic culture in India. Just as it seemed, however, important to educate the Muslims, so also it seemed equally if not more important to convince Europeans of the high standards and flexibility of Islamic civilization. Therefore Syed Ameer Ali published a biography of the Prophet and a history of Islam under the title *The Spirit of Islam* (1897). This book claimed that Islam is not only compatible with progress but is itself progressive. It was widely read in the West.

With the foundation of the Muslim League in 1906, an action in which the Aga Khan was one of the leading spirits, the political representation of Muslims in the subcontinent began. This was an important step as the communalist tensions between Hindus and the Muslim minority increased and hardened, to calm down only for the brief span of World War I and shortly afterwards. Gandhi even supported the so-called *Khilāfat* Movement, an attempt of Indian Muslims to make the Ottoman caliph their spiritual leader. When Ataturk abolished the caliphate in 1924, however, this movement dissolved.

Yet the question "Who is the caliph's legitimate successor?" was discussed time and again in the Muslim world. Sir Muhammad Iqbal, otherwise critical of the laical trends in Turkey and elsewhere, considered the Turkish National Assembly to be the legitimate successor of the Ottoman rulers, without, however, wielding spiritual, let alone, juridical power in other countries. Today, one may think of the ICO, the Islamic Conference Organization, to which belong forty-five states and which can be seen, at least in theory, as a kind of umbrella organization for Muslims.

From the days of the *Khilāfat* Movement a question was asked which became more and more important but was never given a satisfactory answer: "What is an Islamic state?" Terms like democracy and fatherland, *waṭan*, were mentioned in Turkey in the late nineteenth century, very much to the Ottoman sultan's chagrin, but in the twentieth century the problem of what the relation between national interests and all-embracing Islamic aims should be loomed large on the political horizon. Must an Islamic state be ruled by the *sharīʿa*? What would its constitution be? Can it be a democracy? The defenders of democratic ideals find their legitimation in Sura 42/36 where *shūrā*, "council

among people" is mentioned; this was understood as pointing to a democratic system of government.

In the context of reforms one movement that developed in India must be mentioned. That is the Ahmadiyya,
based on the teachings of Mirza Ghulam Ahmad (d. 1908).
In the beginning a very pious and law-abiding Panjabi Muslim, Mirza Ghulam Ahmad claimed, in somewhat unclear
terms though, to be the Mahdi or Messiah. Most Muslims
opposed his ideas fervently from the very beginning as they
seemed to contradict the dogma of the finality of Muhammad's prophethood. In 1953 serious political riots against
the Ahmadiyya took place in Pakistan: the reasons were
probably more social than purely religious because the excellent Ahmadi educational system (typical of a minority)
had resulted in a remarkably high percentage of Ahmadis
occupying leading positions in the country's administration. In the wake of the long conflict, the movement, famed
for its widespread missionary activities in Europe and Africa, was eventually declared "non-Islamic" in 1974.

One of the most outspoken critics of the Ahmadiyya
was the man whom one can call, without exaggeration, the
most fascinating personality among Indian and even among
Muslim reformers. That is Muhammad Iqbal (1877–1938).
Contrary to many other reformers whose weak point was
that they lacked firsthand knowledge of European languages and culture, or at least were aware only of some
fragments of English or French history as offered in the
missionary schools, Iqbal studied philosophy and law in
Cambridge and received his doctorate in Munich with a
remarkable study published as *The Development of Meta-
physics in Persia*. He was deeply steeped in Hegelian
philosophy but later became an admirer of Bergson, Nietzsche, Einstein, and others. Goethe's work impressed him
especially. Iqbal's most important concern was to combine
European thinking with Islamic ideals. He felt that the true
base of Islam is dynamism, an attitude quite contrary to
the classical hellenistic worldview that had super-imposed
itself on Islamic thought just as it had weakened Christianity. (A modern historian of religions will immediately

recognize the contrast between the 'prophetic-dynamic' and the 'mystical-contemplative' attitudes.) Islamic dynamism, says Iqbal, has been concealed for centuries behind fossilized and stifling dogmatics, as well as soporific pantheistic mysticism. The Koran, according to him, teaches the ascension of man to higher and higher realms of experience: man, God's vicegerent on earth, is called to develop his personality, his individuality, in a constant struggle against the powers of evil and to attain gradually the rank of the Perfect Man. Here, the ideals of Muslim mystical leaders are reflected, as is Nietzsche's quest of the Superman. However, Iqbal's ideal Man, the true "man of God," is not distant from God, and even less does he appear, as Nietzsche had claimed, only "after God has died." Rather, this ideal human being exists only according to his relation to God, i.e., as God's servant. To be God's servant is the highest degree of freedom. Was not the Prophet of Islam called *'abduhu,* "His servant" in the two Koranic sentences concerning his highest mystical experiences (Sura 17/1, 53/9)?

The philosophy of the Ego, of the continuous unfolding of the individual's creative powers as preached by Iqbal, is not only the basis for his thoughts about the individual human being but also for his political philosophy. The community too has to utilize and unfold all its inherent possibilities. Only by doing so can it be tolerant (exactly like the individual), for tolerance is the attitude of the strong who respect the other's personality. For Iqbal, Islam is the base and foundation of an ideal state; Islam alone represents unalloyed monotheism and practices the true brotherhood of all believers. In 1928 Iqbal gave a series of talks, published as *Six Lectures on the Reconstruction of Religious Thought in Islam,* in various Indian universities. Here he tried to support and ground his ideas on Islam by skillfully offering Western and Muslim philosophical theories which tie in well with contemporary Christian psychology and the history of religion. However, his thoughts are expressed in a more attractive style in his numerous poetical works, which are written partly in his native Urdu and partly also in Persian, so that they might be distributed better in Iran and the Persian-speaking areas of Asia as well as among Orientalists. Iqbal's *Payām-i mashriq*, "the message of the East," is an answer to Goethe's *West-Östlicher Divan*; Goethe's influence can be seen in many of his poems as well as in his entire world view. The Persian *Jāvīdnāma* is probably Iqbal's most impressive and thought-provoking poem; inspired by Dante's *Divine Comedy*, it describes the soul's journey through the spheres. His guiding companion on the heavenly journey is Maulana Jalaluddin Rumi, who appears in most of Iqbal's poems as his spiritual master. In Rumi's work the Indo-Muslim thinker discovered the truly Islamic idea of a personal God who answers, nay even inspires, man's prayer, and the idea of infinite dynamic Love which lends wings to the seeker to conquer infinite new spiritual horizons. Here, he contradicts many other admirers of Rumi, who usually interpret his verse basing themselves on the philosophical teachings of Ibn ʿArabi's school.

Iqbal offered a fascinating system of thought based on a dynamic Love that transforms the human soul and awakens the slumbering vital powers of Islam and the Muslims. His vision led eventually to the foundation of present-day Pakistan, whose blueprint he had mentioned in 1930 in his presidential address at the annual meeting of the All India Muslim League. Pakistan therefore regards him as its spiritual father, but the influence of his thought and poetry is also palpable in other countries in the Muslim east.

The decades after World War II changed the face of the Islamic world more than the preceding centuries. Pakistan and Libya, Indonesia and the Goldcoast, and many more have become independent states; the Arab countries hold key positions in global politics. The foundation of the state of Israel in 1948, based on the Balfour Declaration of 1917, constitutes an almost insolvable problem for many Islamic countries, and in the perpetually expanding Islamic world one sees many contradictory variants of Islam—once thought to be monolithic. A Belgian Islamologist even goes so far as to speak of "the Muslims and their Islams"—in the plural. Here one sees Ghaddafi's Libya; there the Muslims in Central Asia and China who, deeply influenced by Sufi brotherhoods, dexterously fight the Communist regimes; they have developed a fascinating Muslim culture (including calligraphy) of their own. The stern Wahhabism of Saudi Arabia, which wields a strong influence thanks to worldwide organizations such as the *Rabita,* but also thanks to its seemingly inexhaustible financial resources, can be contrasted with Islam as it appears in Ataturk's laical Turkey. Islam in Southeast Asian countries, introduced centuries ago by speculative mystics and Muslim merchants, is different from Islam in Black Africa, to whose adherents theosophical speculations are rather alien, while 'practical' applications of Muslim ethics seem to prevail, as with the Muridin in Senegal.

Of particular interest is the situation in Turkey. As early as the beginning of this century Zia Gökalp had spoken of "Westernization, Turkization, and Islamization" of Turkey, but Ataturk's reforms after World War I intended a complete break with the country's Islamic past. That was done not only by the substitution of European, mainly Swiss, law for Islamic law, but an even more decisive cultural change came in 1928 with the substitution of the Roman alphabet in place of the Arabic alphabet. After twenty-five years of strictly laical education, the government reintroduced religious classes in schools, and in 1949 founded the Ilâhiyat Fakültesi in Ankara, an Islamic theological Faculty where the future instructors of preachers and *imāms* were trained not only in the classical Islamic sciences but also in modern fields such as comparative history of religion, sociology, and psychology of religion. No comparable institution exists to our knowledge in other Islamic countries. In the course of four decades a number of such faculties were founded in all parts of Turkey—the difference is that in the 1950's the women students did not cover their hair, and now they do.

In Pakistan, the number of religious schools and colleges, often supported by *zakāt* money, has grown considerably during the last ten to twelve years, but liberal, mystical, and fundamentalist forms of Islam stand side by side and vie for educational and political power. The invisible network of the traditional Sufi orders also plays a role in the Pakistani system.

In India, officially a secular country, Muslims seem to feel a certain penchant for Sufism, perhaps because it offers some consolation and spiritual strength to their relatively small population of one hundred million in face of the rising tide of Hindu fundamentalism. Sunni and Shia frictions are not lacking in all parts of the subcontinent.

In Egypt, the pendulum swings in changing directions. One thinks of the former suppression of the Muslim Brethren on the one hand and an increasing return to traditional Islamic values on the other hand. The Muslim Brethren, active mainly in the forties, have well expressed the ideal of the unity of religion and politics in the statement that for them "Islam is faith and worship, fatherland and nation, religion and state, spirituality and activity, Koran and sword." This formulation is probably applicable also to other so-called fundamentalist groups.

In Iran, the revolution of 1979 surprised most western spectators: after attempts at westernization that were urgently implemented by the Pahlavi dynasty, there arose a state ostensibly based on the uncompromising ideals of the Twelver Shia. In judging such developments one must, however, never forget that in many Islamic countries the masses were rather skeptical when it came to an all-too-exaggerated modernization and are still reluctant to accept it wholeheartedly. The theoretical base of post-Pahlavi Iran can be understood in part from the work of 'Ali Shariati, who elaborated, among other ideas, certain formulations of Iqbal. (Incidentally, the Wahhabis in Saudi Arabia largely refuse to accept Iqbal's brand of Islamic reform.)

The emergence of an attitude deemed "fundamentalist" (a word basically meant for certain Christian groups that arose toward the end of the last century in the USA) is understandable and, for the historian of religion, appears almost logical. The entire inherited value system seemed to have lost its importance and been replaced with radically different values under the influence of the West (the influence of western movies and videos cannot be overrated in this process). Now the hope is to find a certain protection from western civilization, or rather its caricatures as marketed in the mass media, by returning to the good old days of the Prophet when things were as they ought to be. Besides, among Muslims, bourgeois liberal ideas had never been formulated in such a way as to attract and offer reliable guidance to the masses, in contrast to the clearcut teachings the fundamentalists. The population in many Islamic countries was confronted with the sad truth that neither liberalism nor socialism was able to solve new political and social problems. Thus, the straight path of Islam and the securely fastened net of inherited ritual and legal traditions remained—or so it seemed to many—the only safe way to salvation here and in the hereafter. One should also not forget that the Islamic languages have no exact term for "secularism": a translation often used in Arabic is *lā dīnī*, which means "non-religious, without religion" and has therefore a strongly negative ring to it. One may mention in passing that in the attempt to harmonize Islam with modern civilization and contemporary trends in politics, some progressive Muslims have not hesitated to depict the Prophet as a socialist, nay, even as a Marxist *avant la lettre*!

A highly important issue for fundamentalists, as for Muslims in general, is the position of women. Is it possible in our day to keep them strictly secluded or locked up? In many Islamic countries there was and still is a considerable number of academically trained women—of women professors, women politicians, and women lawyers—who have worked (for instance in Pakistan) to explain to women their rights as inscribed in Islamic law. In Saudi Arabia, the problem was solved for the time being by founding faculties exclusively for women and banks with exclusively female personnel.

This leads to the problem of Islamic banking, which has been discussed frequently in past years. The Koran prohibits *ribā*, "interest." It is, however, a question whether to apply this prohibition only to excessive usury, as some modernists do, or whether to find other workable strategies to enable Muslims to participate successfully in international business. The old traditions, already treated in medieval legal theory, of sharing profit and loss or feigned sale to circumvent the question of "interest," are still in use today.

The number of Muslim women who study in western universities is high; the fact that Pakistan was led for a short while by a young, Harvard- and Oxford-educated female Prime Minister is remarkable, but it is perhaps even more astounding (though less publicized) that Bangladesh has a woman Prime Minister without a western academic background. Such facts show that there are possibilities for an active role for women in the public sector. Two developments are worthy of attention: among converts to Islam, women outnumber men, and among Muslim women in the West, especially among recent converts, one finds an increasing tendency to follow traditional patterns, for they feel that it is important for them, living in the diaspora, to identify clearly with Islamic ideals. Thus more and more girls (at least in America but, of course, also among the Turks in Europe) wear *hijāb,* the kerchief that covers every hair, and a long coat. Dark glasses serve to avoid eye contact with the other sex.

The stream of immigrants from Muslim countries continues steadily in Europe, be it the guest workers from Turkey with their families in Germany or Indo-Pakistani immigrants in Britain. This adds to the problem of acculturation. Mosques, or at least rooms for congregational prayer, multiply everywhere—London alone has more than eight hundred such places of prayer. The problem of religious instruction for Turkish children in Germany, for North Africans in France and for Indo-Pakistanis in Britain, Canada, and the USA has to be carefully thought out afresh. It should be obligatory for western teachers to have at least some knowledge of Islamic culture and religious values. There is the additional problem of proper diet, since only ritually slaughtered meat, and no pork, is permitted. The most important duty of the immigrants, however, is to introduce the young generation to the cultural heritage of their ancestors. Interestingly, it is often youngsters from the third generation of immigrants who discover anew the attractiveness of their ancestors' culture and languages after a first infatuation with all of Western civilization. In North America, summer camps are organized in which children and teenagers learn, almost in play, something about their own cultural background; Sunni, Twelver Shii, or Ismaili "Sunday" schools are attached to many a mosque.

One of the most active groups in the USA is the Black Muslims who, after inaugural complications, strive to integrate themselves more and more into the traditional Muslim mainstream. It is interesting to see that in some cities (Washington and Houston) they are more successful than the police with drug problems while working with missionary zeal among prisoners. They have been able to attract a number of former criminals to a purer life after repentance.

One aspect common to the so-called fundamentalist currents, whose activities become year by year more obvious, is that only rarely are they interested in the mystical and religious contents of the Koran. Rather they stress the legal, lawbound side of Islam. One can discern a tendency toward demythologization of the Koran among them. The discussion of social and political issues is in the foreground of their preaching while the deep religious mystery of faith is often overlooked.

This attitude is countered by the activity of Sufi brotherhoods. During the last decades multifarious Sufi orders have fascinated European and American seekers, even though (or is it perhaps because?) some of these Sufis are more or less remote from traditional, orthodox Islam and deal with 'Sufi dance' and other forms of devotions which cannot exactly be called Islamic. Yet, besides them several other traditional and traditionalist brotherhoods have established a firm hold in the West. The North African Darqawiyya, a branch of the Shadhiliyya, has attracted a number of members from among highly educated Americans and Europeans. Futhermore, various Sufi centers, especially the Khaniqahs of the Persian Nimatullahi order, are rapidly increasing in number not only in Europe and the United States but even in West Africa and Australia. Some of these centers are involved in publishing works that may make Sufism, and Islam in general, intelligible to a larger reading public, often by new translations of classical Arabic, Persian, and Turkish works and by reprinting earlier translations of such works. It should not be forgotten that a steadily increasing number of Muslim scholars from all parts of the Islamic world is now teaching in western, especially American, universities, specializing in a multitude of fields from physics to business administration.

This situation (as well as conversions to Islam as the result of mixed marriages) creates new problems, e.g.,how to lead a truly Islamic life in the diaspora. The relation of Muslims, who constitute a numerical minority in many countries, with a majority which may be only slightly larger, is often strained. As many Muslims, especially in the Third World, believe that numerical strength is important for the success of Islam, one finds the tendency to have large families (India and Central Asia are prime examples), and the increase in birth rate is difficult to curb even though Islamic law permits birth control.

The Islamic world is undergoing a process of change. It is therefore impossible to predict exactly what its future and its future role will be. One may remind the reader of the Koranic saying which was quoted over and again by the modernists: "Verily God does not change the fate of a people unless the people change what is in themselves." (Sura 13/12).

The student of Islamic culture can only hope that the kind of dynamic Islam preached by leaders like Iqbal may give new vital impulses to the different Muslim peoples and lead them toward a bright future in which the true values of Islam are realized. But how do humans change in such a direction? By entrusting themselves to the guidance of God, who has revealed Himself in the word of the Koran; by striving for unification of one's own small will with the Divine Will, for the destinies He has in store are infinite as He Himself is infinite; by accepting Divine wisdom and performing one's duties; by recognizing God's all-embracing rule as well as His incomprehensibility, for:

> He is God besides whom there is no deity, the One who knows the visible and the invisible. He is the Merciful, the Compassionate. He is God besides whom there is no deity, the King, the Holy, the Giver of Peace, the Faithful, the Protector, the Mighty, the Overpowering, the Very High. Glory be to God who is above what they associate with Him. He is God, the Creator, the Form-giver; His are the Most Beautiful Names. Whatever is in the heavens and on earth glorifies Him, and He is the Mighty, the Wise. (Sura 59/23–24)

Select Bibliography

In the last twenty years the literature on Islam has grown dramatically, through works written by Muslims, as well as through sociological studies, research on specific questions, and works on art and music history. Only a few titles can be mentioned here:

Ahmed, Akbar S., *Discovering Islam: Making Sense of Muslim History and Society*, London and New York, 1988.

Ali, Syed Ameer, *The Spirit of Islam*, London, 1922.

An Historical Atlas of Islam, edited by William Brice, Leiden, 1981.

Andrae, Tor, *In the Garden of Myrtles: Studies in Early Islamic Mysticism*, translated from the Swedish by Birgitta Sharpe, foreword by Annemarie Schimmel, with a biographical introduction by Eric Sharpe, Albany, 1988.

Arberry, Arthur J., *Aspects of Islamic Civilization*, Ann Arbor, 1967.

————— . *The Koran interpreted,* 2 vols., London and New York, 1955.

————— . (editor), *Religion in the Middle East,* 2 vols., Cambridge, 1969.

Arnold, Sir Thomas, *The Preaching of Islam,* London, 1898.

Bausani, Alessandro, *Persia Religiosa,* Milan, 1959.

Bell's Introduction to the Qurʾan, completely revised and enlarged by W. Montgomery Watt, Edinburgh, 1970.

Bousquet, Georges-Henri (editor), *al-Ghazālī, Ihyāʾ ʿUlūm al-Dīn or Vivification des sciences de la foi,* Paris, 1955. [Analysis and index with the collaboration of a team of Arabists.]

————— . *Les grandes pratiques rituelles de l'Islam,* Paris, 1949.

Calverley, Edwin Elliott, *Worship in Islam,* London 1947, reprinted in 1957.

Chittick, William, *The Sufi Path of Knowledge: Ibn ʿArabi,* Albany, 1989.

————— . *The Sufi Path of Love: The Spiritual Teachings of Rumi* Albany, 1983.

Le Coran, interlinear (French) translation and notes by Muhammad Hamidullah, Paris, 1959.

Le Coran, (French) translation by Regis Blachère, 3 vols., Paris, 1947–51.

Corbin, Henry, *L'homme de lumière dans le soufisme iranien,* Paris, 1971. German translation by Annemarie Schimmel: Die smaragdene Vision. Der Lichtmensch im iranischen Sufismus, Munich, 1989. English translation by Nancy Pearson: *The Man of Light in Iranian Sufism,* Boulder and New York, 1978.

Cragg, Kenneth, *The Call of the Minaret,* New York, 1956.

————— . *The Event of the Qurʾān: Islam in its Scripture,* London, 1971.

————— . *The Pen and the Faith: Eight Modern Muslim Writers and the Quran,* London and Boston, 1985.

[All works by Kenneth Cragg are stimulating and interesting.]

Denny, Frederick Mathewson, *An Introduction to Islam*, New York and London, 1985.

Dictionary of Islam, ed. A. J. Wensinck and J. H. Kramers, Leiden, 1941.

Donaldson, Dwight M., *The Shiite Religion*, London, 1933.

Eaton, Charles Le Gai, *Islam and the Destiny of Man*, Cambridge and London, 1985.

Encyclopedia of Islam, New edition, Leiden, 1960–. Leiden and New York.

Ende, Werner and Steinbach, Udo (editors), *Der Islam in der Gegenwart*, second edition, Munich, 1989.

Endress, Gerhard, *Introduction to Islam*, translated by Carole Hillenbrand, Edinburgh, 1988.

Esposito, John, *Islam: The Straight Path*, New York, 1988, 1991.

Gardet, Louis and Anawati, C. G., *Introduction à la théologie musulmane*, Paris, 1948.

Gaudefroy-Demombynes, Jean, *La pélérinage à la Mekke*, Paris, 1923.

Geertz, Clifford, *Islam Observed*, New Haven, 1968.

Gerholm, Tomas and Lithman, Yngve George (editors), *The New Islamic Presence in Western Europe*, London and New York, 1988.

Gibb, Sir Hamilton A. R., *Mohammedanism*, London, New York, Toronto, 1953.

Goldziher, Ignaz, *Muslim Studies*, edited by S. M. Stern, translated from the German by C. R. Barbar and S. M. Stern, 2 vols., Chicago, 1968–71.

———. *Mohammed and Islam*, translated from the German by Kate Chambers Seelye, with an introdution by Morris Jastrow, Jr., New Haven, 1917.

Gramlich, Richard, *Die schiitischen Derwischorden Persiens*, 3 vols., Wiesbaden, 1965–80.

———. *Die Wunder der Freunde Gottes: Theologien und Erscheinungsformen des islamischen Heiligenwunders*, Stuttgart, 1987.

Haarmann, Ulrich, *Geschichte der arabischen Welt*, Munich, 1987.

Halm, Heinz, *Die Schia*, Darmstadt, 1988.

Hamidullah, Muhammad, *Le Prophète de l'Islam*, 2 vols., Paris, *1959*.

Hartmann, Richard, *Die Religion des Islam: Eine Ein-führung*, Berlin, 1944, reprinted in Darmstadt, 1992.

Hodgson, Marshall, *The Venture of Islam*, 3 vols., Chicago, 1975.

Husain, Freda (editor), *Muslim Women*, New York, 1984.

Ibn Hishām, ʿAbd al-Malik, *The Life of Muhammad*, a translation of Ibn Ishāq's *Sīrat Rasūl Allah* by A. Guillaume, Lahore, 1955.

Jäschke, Gotthard, *Der Islam in der neuen Türkei*, Leiden, 1951.

Jomier, Jacques, *How to Understand Islam*, New York, 1989.

Kassis, Hanna E., *A Concordance of the Qurʾan*, with a foreword by Fazlur Rahman, Berkeley, 1983.

Keddie, Nikki R. (editor), *Scholars, Saints and Sufis: Muslim Religious Institutions Since 1500*, Berkeley, 1972.

Der Koran, (German) translation by Max Henning, introduction and notes by Annemarie Schimmel, Stuttgart, 1960, 1991.

Der Koran, (German) translation by Rudi Paret, 2 vols.: Vol. 1, Translation, Stuttgart, 1962, reprinted in 1982; Vol. 2, Commentary and Concordance, Stuttgart, 1971, reprinted in 1977.

Der Koran, (German) translation by Friedrich Rückert, Frankfurt, 1888, reprinted in Hildesheim, 1980.

Lewis, Bernard (editor), *Islam and the Arab World*, New York, 1976.

Lings, Martin, *The Quranic Art of Calligraphy and Illumination*, New York, 1987.

MacCarthy, Richard, *The Theology of al-Ashʿari*, Cambridge and Toronto, 1953.

————. *Freedom and Fulfillment*, Boston, 1978. [Translation of various works of al-Ghazzali].

Makdisi, George, *Religion, Law and Learning in Classical Islam*, Hampshire and Brookfield, 1991.

Martin, Richard C. (editor), *Islam in Local Contexts*, Leiden, 1982.

Massignon, Louis, *La Passion d'al-Hosayn Ibn Mansûr al-Hallaj, martyre mystique de l'Islam*, 2 vols., Paris, 1922, reprinted in 4 volumes in Paris, 1975. English translation, Princeton, 1982.

Molé, Marijan, *Les mystiques musulmans*, Paris, 1965.

Morgan, Kenneth (editor), *Islam: The Straight Path. Islam Interpreted by Muslims*, New York, 1958.

Mottahedeh, Roy, *The Mantle of the Prophet: Religion and Politics in Iran*, New York, 1985.

Mutahhari, Murtaza, *The Islamic Modest Dress*, translated from Persian by Laleh Bakhtiar, Albequerque, 1988.

Nasr, Seyyid Hossein, *Islam: Ideals and Realities*, London, 1966.

——. *Science and Civilization in Islam*, Cambridge, 1968.

Nelson, Kristina, *The Art of Reciting the Qur'an*, Austin, 1985.

Nicholson, Reynold A., *Studies in Islamic Mysticism*, Cambridge, 1921.

Nöldeke, Theodor, *Geschichte des Korans*, 2 vols., Leipzig, 1860, second edition Leipzig 1909–38, reprinted in Hildesheim, 1961.

Nurbakhsh, Javad, *Sufi Symbolism: The Nurbakhsh Encyclopedia of Sufi Terminology*, translated by Leonard Lewisohn and Terry Graham, London, 1986–.

Padwick, Constance E., *Muslim Devotions*, London, 1960.

Pickthall, Marmaduke, *The Meaning of the Glorious Koran*, New York, 1953.

Popovic, Alexandre and Veinstein, Gilles (editors), *Les ordres mystiques dans l'Islam: Cheminements et situation actuelle*, Paris, 1986. (Recherches d'histoire et de sciences sociales. 13.)

Rahman, Fazlur, *Islam, London, 1966*.

——. *Major Themes of the Qur'ān, Minneapolis, 1980*.

Readings in the Qur'an: A Contemporary Translation, Princeton, 1988.

Ritter, Helmut: *Das Meer der Seele: Mensch, Welt und Gott in den Geschichten des Farīd ud-dīn ʿAṭṭār, Leiden, 1955.*

Schacht, Joseph, *The Origins of Muhammadan Jurisprudence,* Oxford, 1950.

Schimmel, Annemarie: *And Muhammad Is His Messenger,* Chapel Hill, 1986.

————. *Calligraphy and Islamic Culture,* New York, 1984, 1989.

————. *Gabriel's Wing: A Study into the Religious Ideas of Sir Muhammad Iqbal,* Leiden, 1963, Lahore, 1989.

————. *I Am Wind, You Are Fire: The Life and Work of Rumi,* Boston, 1992

————. *Islam in the Indian Subcontinent,* Leiden, 1980.

————. *Islamic Names,* Edinburgh, 1989.

————. *Mystical Dimensions of Islam,* Chapel Hill, 1975, several editions, revised 1990.

————. *The Triumphal Sun: A Study of Mowlana Jalaloddin Rumi's Work,* London and the Hague, 1978.

Smith, W. Cantwell, *Islam in Modern History,* Princeton, 1957.

Trimingham, J. Spencer, *The Sufi Orders in Islam,* Oxford, 1971.

Yusuf Ali, A., *The Holy Quran,* New edition, Lahore, 1977.

Waardenburg, Jacques (editor), *Islam, ideal en werkelijkheid,* Antwerp, 1984. [With an outstanding bibliography for further reading.]

Walther, Wiebke, *Die Frau im Islam,* Stuttgart, 1980.

Watt, W. Montgomery, *Muhammad: Prophet and Statesman,* London, 1964, reprinted 1969.

————. *Free Will and Predestination,* London, 1948.

————. *Muhammad at Mekka,* Oxford, 1953.

————. *Muhammad at Medina,* Oxford, 1956.

Von Grunebaum, Gustave E., *Muhammadan Festivals,* introduction by C. E. Bosworth, New York, 1988.

Wensinck, Arent Jan, *A Handbook of Early Muhammadan Tradition,* Leiden, 1927.

Index